WAYS TO PRAY

WAYS TO PRAY
SERMONS NO. 4

THOMAS SHAW, SSJE
EDITOR

CAMBRIDGE, MASSACHUSETTS

International Standard Book No.: 0-936384-19-0
Library of Congress Catalog No.: 84-071180

Published in the United States of America by Cowley Publications
Cover designed by James Madden, SSJE

PREFACE

From individuals who are unfamiliar with the Society of St.
John the Evangelist often comes the question, "What is it that you
do as a religious community?" I expect they are asking if we are
essentially teachers, or if we staff parishes, or administer retreat
centers. All these are certainly traditional responsibilities for
religious communities. What does come to mind, of course, is
our ministry of the Word in preaching, in publishing, giving
retreats, and teaching. Or what comes to mind is our pastoral
ministry of spiritual direction and counseling. Or our ministry
of hospitality.

And yet, valid as those responses might be, they are not the
heart of what we do as a religious community. For fundamentally
what we believe we are called together by God to do, as all Christians are, is to seek, corporately and individually, an ever deepening relationship with God our creator in prayer. If our ministry is
to be truly a manifestation of the Spirit's power in the world,
then it must first be born in and then nurtured with God.

Now, perhaps more than ever before in the life of the Church,
lay people are seeking to reclaim and identify their Christian
ministry. Ordained clergy, too, face considerable confusion in
adapting the traditional ministries of priesthood and the diaconate
to the Church that the Spirit is always calling to renewal and
refreshment. Where do we find the answers? How do we solve
these problems? We believe it is through exercising the gift of
prayer given to every Christian, religious, lay or ordained, in our
common baptism. And that is the reason we offer this latest
volume of Cowley sermons on prayer to you.

You will not find in these sermons a tidy technique or method
of prayer. For prayer is relationship; if a relationship is growing
and maturing it is necessarily untidy and incomplete. Nor will you
find all, or even most of the answers to the problems you face in

your own life with God, for true relationships are by their nature unique, as individual as you are or as I am.

What you will find in these sermons are the experiences with God in prayer of five men and one woman. How one person experiences forgiveness from God, and how another expresses his desire for God. How another feels the presence of God as he grows older, and so on. It is our hope that the testimony of their experience may give you some insight into your own relationship with God, and that these sermons might raise some new questions for you, provide an opening for you, or give a measure of relief to you in what is often an arduous and confusing enterprise. But, most of all, we hope these sermons will encourage you to pray and will give you confidence in your own prayer.

All but one of these sermons are by members of the Society of St. John the Evangelist. We thought it was appropriate to include a sermon by Sister Ann Goggin, rc in this collection of Cowley sermons on prayer because she has been, through her teaching, her spiritual direction, and her conduct of retreats so intimately involved in the spiritual growth of our own community.

Thomas Shaw, SSJE

CONTENTS

WAYS TO PRAY

THE JESUS PRAYER

Wide and long Christian experience keeps before us two expectations in the field of prayer. First, it encourages us to spell out our real needs to God, praying about what is concrete and particular; and, similarly, encourages us to express our thankfulness in detail about real experiences and events that we accept as gifts from God. The Scriptures teach that generalized moods or intentions aren't enough; inertia tends to hold us back from fully engaged prayer. So we are urged to ask, knock, and seek. "Have no anxiety about anything. In everything by prayer and supplication with thanksgiving make your requests known to God" (Phil. 4:6).

Secondly, we are led to expect that we will grow in the capacity for a prayer of intimacy in which our meaning and intention is conveyed very simply, in a few words. A similar development is a common experience in human relationships. As we know another person better we begin to communicate intuitively, and particular words or phrases may come to acquire all sorts of resonances and harmonies and associations arising from common experience. People who know and love each other deeply can communicate in a few words which have become almost a code. While never forsaking articulate prayer of asking and thanking, we find that much of our praying simplifies itself. We simply pray "O God, help!" St. Francis once prayed all night, repeating, "My God and my all"; in a lesser way, we find ourselves praising God or depending on him in a few words said over and over again.

If it has been our practice to meditate on the scriptures, we come in time to be drawn less and less to teasing out the meaning of the passage and its relevance to our life in detail. Instead there is a tendency for one word or phrase to "light up" or reverberate in such a way that we want to hold it in our attention, ruminating, listening, absorbing, savoring. "Behold the Lamb of God! This is my beloved Son, listen to him. I am the Bread of Life." We find ourselves gently repeating the words. At this time we are likely to be growing in an increased trust in the unconscious parts of ourselves, becoming aware that vastly significant things can be going on within us at a level deeper than conscious rational thought or 'conversational' prayer. "Likewise the Spirit helps us in our weakness; for we do not know how to pray as we ought, but the Spirit himself intercedes for us with sighs too deep for words. And he who searches human hearts knows what is the mind of the Spirit, because the Spirit intercedes for the saints according to the will of God" (Rom. 8: 26-27).

In this age when everything tends to be made a matter of technique, it is worth emphasizing that non-conversational, non-discursive prayer is something that is *given*; it arises in the course of our personal relationship with God. It is not a method which we arbitrarily adopt and implement out of ambition, or in a self-conscious way. However, when a person is rooted in the sacra-mental life of the Church, reads and thinks about the scriptures, listens to homilies and discusses the faith in earnest with others, this simplified, direct, non-conversational prayer may be appro-priate and right. Faith is stimulated and developed in a number of ways in prayer. There can now be the deliberate intention of centering on God, maintaining our attention to him in a continu-ous movement of love by means of the repetition of a single word or sentence.

There is no one single name for this kind of praying. We might call it 'prayer of loving attention sustained by the repeti-tion of a word.' It has been called 'rhythm prayer,' which points to the rhythmic nature of this repetition; something natural and free, not mechanical and obsessive like incantation. The early monastic teachers called it *monologistos*—"single-worded"—prayer and the appeal 'O God make speed to save me, O Lord make haste to help me' at the beginning of offices derives from this tradition. Contemporary teachers have coined the term 'center-ing prayer,' pointing to the inner heart of the person as the 'place' of this praying. In this prayer, the mind is united with the deep center, the heart. The term suggests the unifying integrating quality of the prayer. It suggests to me the image of the potter, too. Some sort of a pot can be made by prodding and squeezing a lump of clay, but usually the result is uneven and misshapen. But if the clay is centered on the turning wheel as the potter's hand squeezes it, then a pot can be simply and gracefully formed.

We ought to lay to rest here misgivings about repetition arising from Jesus warnings against "vain repetition" in the gospels. Actually the King James Version is not helpful here. The Greek does not refer to repetition as such, but almost certainly to the quasi-magical prayer of incantation, the manipulation of God by the elaborate recitation of many divine names and sacred phraseology.

One obvious appeal of this kind of centering prayer is its real simplicity and ease. It is available equally to the clever and the simple; there is no intricate method to follow, and no special circumstances required. However at another level it is quite hard and testing. There is a real poverty to this form of prayer; it is a stripping down. In this kind of prayer, tradition tells us, we are not to conjure up any kind of mental pictures. Nor are we to pursue and develop any thoughts which crop up, even ones which seem impressively spiritual. "Prayer," wrote Evagrius of Pontus, "is a laying aside of thoughts." We notice that his language, though firm, is gentle—he speaks of laying aside, not violently suppressing.

One of the best-known expositions of the contemplative prayer we are talking about is *The Cloud of Unknowing*, a classic of medieval English spirituality. These are typical words of wisdom from the book: "So when you feel by the grace of God that he is calling you to this work and you intend to respond, lift your heart to God with humble love. And really mean God Himself who created you and brought you and graciously called you to this state of life. And think no other thought of Him. It all depends on your desire. A naked intention directed to God and himself alone, is wholly sufficient.

"If you want this intention summed up in a word to retain it more easily, take a short word, preferably of one syllable, to do

so. The shorter the word the better, more like the working of the
spirit. A word like *God* or *Love*. . . . And fix this word fast to
your heart, so that it is always there, come what may. It will be
your shield and spear in peace and war alike. With this word you
will hammer the cloud and the darkness above you. With this
word you will suppress all thoughts under the cloud of forgetting.
So much so that if ever you are tempted to think what it is that
you are seeking, this one word will be sufficient answer. . . ."

In the Eastern Church a gradual process of development
from the fifth to the tenth centuries brought into special prom-
inence one formula of prayer. This is the "Jesus Prayer," an
invocation whose classic form is "Lord Jesus Christ, Son of God,
have mercy on me." A vast and rich literature—for example, the
collection of texts called the *Philokalia*—witnesses to the central
place this has occupied in Orthodox churches, especially in monastic circles. Its use has generated a great interest amongst western
Christians since the emigration of many Orthodox Christians at
the time of the Russian Revolution.

The standard form admits of variations, such as the addition
of the words "a sinner" at the end; it is also a widespread practice
to reduce the prayer to the name alone—Jesus. Why has this form
of prayer become so highly prized? First, the prayer is one of
personal encounter with the living, risen Christ. It makes unequiv-
ocally clear the fact that Christian meditation is not geared to the
attainment of some inner state, however beneficial, as in so-called
'transcendental' meditation. It is not the incantation of a
mantra. It is a living act of personal faith and trust in Jesus Christ,
who is human and divine. It renders that unconditional love and
praise of which St. Paul spoke: "At the name of Jesus every knee
should bow in heaven and on earth and under the earth and every
tongue confess that Jesus Christ is Lord to the glory of God the
Father" (Phil. 2:10f). This phrase, 'to the glory of God the
Father,' is important, for the prayer is valued for its implicit Trini-
tarian nature. It does not involve some sort of fixation on Jesus;
the prayer calling Jesus 'Son of God' leads on to speak of God the

Father: "No one comes to the Father except by me." Equally we are depending on the Holy Spirit in the Jesus Prayer, for as St. Paul says, "No one can say Jesus is Lord except by the Holy Spirit."

Secondly, the Jesus Prayer is prized because, in the words of Kallistos Ware, "it embraces the two chief 'moments' of Christian devotion: the 'moment' of adoration, of waking up to God's glory and reaching out to Him in love, and the 'moment' of penitence, the sense of unworthiness and sin. There is a circular movement within the prayer, a sequence of ascent and return. In the first half of the prayer we rise up to God, with 'Lord Jesus Christ, Son of God,' and in the second half we return to ourselves in compunction with, 'Have mercy on me, a sinner.' "

In the practice of the prayer, no special techniques are involved. Experience shows that the prayer can become linked with a natural rhythm of breathing in and out without self-conscious striving. We are invited to simply begin by calling on the Holy Spirit and then lovingly pray the Name. "Do not think that you are invoking the Name; think only of Jesus Himself. Say his Name slowly and quietly," writes an anonymous Orthodox exponent of the Jesus Prayer. He tells us to lay aside the wish to associate the invocation of the Holy Name with inner intensity or emotion. Any kind of force is inappropriate. Another important point is that the rhythm of repetition is not an incessant or continuous one. "The Name pronounced may be extended and prolonged in seconds or minutes of silent rest and attention. The repetition of the Name may be likened to the beating of wings by which a bird rises into the air. It must never be laboured and forced, or hurried. It must be gentle, easy, and—let us give to this word its deepest meaning—graceful. When the bird has reached the desired height it glides in its flight, and only beats its wings from time to time in order to stay in the air. So the soul, having attained to the thought of Jesus and filled herself with the memory of him may discontinue the repetition of the Name and rest in our Lord. The repetition will only be resumed when other thoughts threaten to crowd out the thought of Jesus."

If we pray the Jesus Prayer regularly for whatever lengths of time are appropriate to us (twenty minutes or half an hour is about right for most, and more is not recommended for beginners) we soon find the prayer spontaneously rising up from time to time during the day. It has a way of reorienting us after some backsliding or forgetfulness of God. Pronouncing the Name over what we see and experience and value has a transfiguring effect as we recognize the universal presence of Christ, who ascended "that He might fill all things," and give expression to praise and thanksgiving. And in pronouncing the Name inwardly over those we encounter we surround them with blessing, lift them up in intercession, and acknowledge Christ as present in the depths of every person.

Martin Smith, SSJE

THE PRAYER OF THE HEART

Martin Smith began this series by speaking of the process of getting through to the heart by means of the Jesus Prayer. Tonight we are going to consider the relationship between heart and Word, and how the heart is laid bare to the creative power of the word of God, while the other faculties are quieted for awhile and wait in patience.

I want to start with a passage from Chaim Potok's novel, *In the Beginning*. Potok is describing the experience of a young Orthodox Jew named David Laurie as he attends the local synagogue on the eve of a Jewish festival.

I remember one night when we danced with the Torah scrolls in our little synagogue. It was the night of Simchat Torah, the festival that celebrates the completion of the annual cycle of Torah readings. The last portion of the Five Books of Moses would be read the next morning. The little synagogue was crowded and tumultuous with joy. I remember one white bearded Torah-reader dancing with one of the heavy scrolls, as if he had miraculously shed his years. My father and my uncle danced for what seemed an interminable length of time, circling about one another, rocking their scrolls, advancing upon one another with their scrolls, backing off, singing. Saul, and Alex, and I danced too. I relinquished my Torah to someone in the crowd, and went out the rear door to the back porch, and let the air cool my face. The noise and dancing came clearly through the open windows; and undulating, swelling and receding, and thinning and growing and receding, and thinning and growing sound. The joy of dancing with Torah, rocking it and holding it close to your heart, the very Words of God. I wondered if Gentiles ever danced with their Bible. Hey, Tony and Eddie: do you ever rock it and hold it and know how much you love it?

10

This, I think, is what we are about tonight. We are considering our own rocking and dancing with the word of God, the guarding and the savoring that goes on when the word of God accosts our hearts, and suddenly the one recognizes the other—as when Jesus turned suddenly and looked at Levi in the Tax Office, or when he revealed himself to Mary Magadalene at the empty tomb. A spark is made from heart to Word, and a profound dialogue begins. The word of God, says the letter to the Hebrews, is a sharp, two-edged sword, piercing between joint and marrow, and creating new life within us.

This creative process begins as we take in the word of God, and "chew it," as Martin described. The heart takes in the Word, consumes it, and digests it, as Ezekiel ate the scroll before his mission to the house of Israel. We harbor the Word in our hearts; we cherish it and cling to it; we toss it to and fro in our hearts, and we murmur it day and night. The word of God and our hearts must become at home with each other, as the letter to the Colossians says. The more frequently the Word makes itself heard, the longer the heart keeps vigil and stays awake; the more attentively the heart listens to the Word, the deeper it penetrates into our innermost being. We are describing the monastic practice of *lectio divina*.

The early Fathers refer to these goings on as *mediatatio*, not meaning "meditation" in the sense of pious reflection, but rather in the more ancient sense of constant repetition, a persistent murmuring of the words. The Desert Fathers called this activity the "rocking of the heart"; the heart rises and falls like a ship on the waves, and it tosses and tumbles the Word in order to make it its own. The medieval monks often used the word *ruminare* to indicate the *chewing* of the Word, evoking the image of a cow settling down under a tree and patiently and incessantly chewing its cud.

This is the prelude to praying with the Bible. The cud that I am mulling over is no human word, but God's word, and it could at any moment strike root and germinate.

I may be listening to God's word at the Eucharist, at the daily office, or in my own private reading, when suddenly I am struck by a particular phrase or word that strikes me. I dwell upon it and stand guard over it. I take it over and over, repeating it slowly in the interior region of my heart. I rock it to and fro, and I ruminate upon it, or chew it over. I allow it to sink into my heart and to flush out everything else.

Here we rub shoulders with the Jesus Prayer, for the Name above every name is the Word par excellence. Vigilance with the Word and the Jesus Prayer go together, supporting and complementing one another. The Jesus Prayer, in fact, developed from the practice in Cassian's time of reciting Biblical verses over and over in the heart.

> O God make speed to save me
>
> O Lord make haste to help me

In this quiet state, we are at the beginning of prayer. The heart has been awakened; it hears the voice of Jesus Christ and rejoices in his word. The Word has been turned over and over in the heart; it has cleansed and purified us and we have grown familiar with it. Perhaps we are even beginning to resemble this Word, so that it becomes the word of God in our flesh, taking root in the heart and bearing fruit.

In this quiet state the Word may achieve its glorious course and give birth to prayer; at that point, it becomes truly our own. It has been chewed over and assimilated, and it is now regenerated in the heart to the praise of God. We now utter the Word and sent it back to God. It has taken root in our innermost being and become our response to the love of the Father. The Spirit stammers it out, and it flows over like water: it is no longer we who pray, but the prayer prays itself within us. Then the word of God can be said to dwell in us richly, for in it we are rooted and grounded; by it we order our lives; all the while we overflow with praise and thanksgiving.

I thought we might use the Gospel appointed for today as an example of what can happen with this kind of prayer. Jesus goes to a sacred pool, or spring, where a congregation of the sick and the blind are assembled because of the pool's healing power. In the midst of this scene of despair mingled with hope lies an isolated cripple, who also desires to be healed, but who has no real hope of reaching the pool. Jesus initiates a dialogue with this man, heals him, and commands him to carry his bed through the crowd, the Sabbath notwithstanding.

We know that this story has parallels in the Synoptics, and that in spite of several peculiarities in John's version the story seems to stem from the primitive tradition about Jesus. But during this prayer time I am not going to worry too much as to whether or not this Gospel reflects the tension between Jews and Christians in the early second century, or whether it reflects an actual controversy between Jesus and the Jewish authorities a century earlier. I am going to allow my critical faculties to rest and wait for awhile in patience, while I allow the risen Christ to stand before me in this gospel and give free rein to my imagination.

I start by quieting myself in the presence of God and begin to read the passage until I hit upon a word or phrase that attracts me, and then I stop:

When Jesus saw him, and knew that he had been lying there a long time, he said to him: 'Do you want to be healed?'

I am gripped by this question and begin to hear it as if it were addressed to me. Then my reading, my *lectio*, stops, and my *meditatio* begins. I take the phrase and repeat it over and over. I don't answer the question immediately, but simply keep repeating the words, slowly, reducing my reflection to a minimum. "Jesus saw him, and said: 'Do you want to be healed?' " I allow the words to sink into my heart and mind, and to become a part of me:

"Jesus saw him, and said; 'Do you want to be healed?' "

As I do this, I begin gradually to savor and relish the words I am repeating. I feel myself more and more in a state of quiet; I feel saturated by the words, and touched by the healing they give. This is the time to stop the *meditatio* and to begin my prayer, the *oratio*. I begin to speak spontaneously with the risen Lord, in whose presence I am, by making his dialogue with the paralytic my own, or I might simply maintain a loving silence in his presence, filled as I am with the attitude that these words have induced in me. I may proceed,

Lord, you know everything; you know that I wish to be healed.

But I hear the words repeated:

James, do you really wish to be healed?

The words resound in my whole being, and challenge me and awaken me, provoking a new response. I may continue:

Lord, what is this healing you speak of? I have come to you for healing many times in the past, and you have not done it. Is there perhaps some block that prevents me from knowing it?

Perhaps at some level I'm beginning to reflect that perhaps I have forgotten that I am not a person divided into body and soul, but a whole individual, whose emotions and body very much affect my mind and spirit. Perhaps I have forgotten that salvation is for the whole person and that Jesus brings life in every possible dimension.

At any rate, I pray in this fashion, or I simply continue in loving silence as long as I can without being distracted. When I notice that I am finding it hard to maintain this prayer without distraction, I pick up my text and start again.

St. Benedict told his monks, *"Oratio sit brevis et pura*, Let prayer be brief and pure." He was not speaking of the time given to prayer and meditation in general, but rather of this third part of prayer that we have described, the *oratio*, which should be held on to as long as it is pure, that is, without distraction. When the distractions appear, it is time to continue the *lectio*.

The place of the psalms in this type of prayer is obvious; the psalm comes into being at the very instant when the heart, having taken in the Word of God, utters that word anew in the guise of prayer. The Spirit in which Jesus prayed and recreated the psalms is poured out on every baptized person, who in the same Spirit can make the psalm his or her own and pray it anew. The psalms and the gospels form an immense storehouse for this kind of praying, and can be used as back-up material; or I can form my own words, as I listen to my heart and the Holy Spirit stirring within.

Lord, that I may see . . . Lord, you know everything; you know that I love you . . . Lord, I believe, help my unbelief . . .

and so on. The list is endless, and each word, each saying, is inexhaustible in the light and in the power of the Holy Spirit. So long as one of these formulas keeps my heart in motion, I hold on to it and quietly persist. Perhaps I will try as well to breathe in the rhythm of my phrases; in this way, my body's resonance will answer to the pulse-beat of my prayer. I breathe back to God the word of God that the Spirit has breathed out to me in Scripture, and perhaps here I will fall back for a time upon the Jesus Prayer which is one among many possibilities.

Two warnings about all that has been said. I am not talking about some magic formula that is going to set our hearts on fire every time we pray. How many times have I been told, "James, it doesn't work!" This process of *lectio divina* that I have been describing entails many times of dryness, and persistent reading through material that may seem useless at the time, but through patient reading of Scripture, both on my own, or perhaps through some form of prayer based on the daily office. I am building up that storehouse of sayings, invitations, questions, and challenges that may eventually come into play in some immediate situation. From the psalms, for instance,

> I have waited for the Lord:
> He stoops to me and hears my cry . . .

or from the Gospels, sayings such as

> Launch out into the deep . . .
>
> What I do you know not now:
> But you shall know hereafter . . . .

I may have passed by these phrases many times before; suddenly they germinate and take root within me, and speak profoundly to my immediate situation.

We should remember, too, that these interior goings-on are no private affair between God and myself. The whole world is involved in it because prayer is a cosmic enterprise, for which some are freer than others. In my prayer I have become a free human being. The word of God has been able to reverberate in my inmost center, and this should be a source of light and power for others. In my experience of prayer, the world's spatial limits are changed, and whether I am far off or close at hand no longer matters very much, for in my prayer I am at one and the same time separated from everyone and bound up with everyone. As André Louf reminds us, "The deepest depth of my heart is also the deep ground of the whole world."

James Madden, SSJE

THE LORD'S PRAYER

The Lord's Prayer is the prayer par excellence of the Christian community. It has a place at every Eucharist and is recited at all the Prayer Book offices and services. Children learn it and stumble over its words long before they understand what they are saying, and this has given rise to anecdotes passed on from generation to generation. Perhaps there really was a child who thought that God's name was Harold. Perhaps there really were children in New York who prayed: Lead us not into Penn Station.

If so, this is not all bad. Folk religion has a role to play; while it is not enough, it is better than nothing and is often a preparation for a fuller and richer faith. The Lord's Prayer becomes imbedded in the mind and surfaces at times of crisis in later life, only to take on a real and deeper meaning. Edwin Muir, the great Scottish poet, wrote in his autobiography: "I suddenly found myself . . . reciting the Lord's Prayer in a loud, emphatic voice— a thing I had not done for many years—with deep urgency and profound . . . emotion. . . . Now, I realized that . . . I was a Christian, no matter how bad a one."

In spite of the role of the Lord's Prayer in our piety, the version in St. Luke's Gospel comes as a shock when we hear it read from one of the modern translations, translations which are based on better and more ancient manuscripts than the ones in the King James Bible and the former Books of Common Prayer. Listen to the prayer, once more, as it is found in the Revised Standard Version of the Bible:

> Father,
> Hallowed be thy name.
> Thy kingdom come.
> Give us each day our daily bread;
> Forgive us our sins, for we ourselves forgive
>   every one who is indebted to us;
> And lead us not into temptation.

The Standing Liturgical Commission would have really been in trouble if it had presented this translation for trial use, but it is authentic. Scholars tell us that it is not a shortened form of the Lord's Prayer as we find it in St. Matthew's gospel, but a completely independent and earlier version. If this version comes as a shock, its original meaning will be even more so after we have stripped away the layers of meaning which have adhered to it over the centuries.

The austere address to God in St. Luke's version of the Lord's Prayer takes us back to something unique in Jesus' teaching. "Our Father" and even "my Father" are not unknown in Judaism, but "Father" by itself seems to be unique to Jesus, especially in the form "abba" that has survived in Aramaic in the writings of St. Mark and St. Paul, even when almost every other word has been expressed in the vernacular of the day. "Abba, Father" is closer even to Daddy or Papa. It expresses an intimacy with God which was not encouraged in ancient Israel. It presupposes a degree of intimacy which translators find difficult to express in modern English, and which would certainly be felt to be inappropriate by many church people.

The phrase "Hallowed be thy name" also presents problems. At one time, the Prayer Book revisors tried "Holy be your name," which was rightly rejected; it won't work. Certainly the sense of the original is not the meaning given to the phrase in popular usage: God's name is to be kept holy. This misses the point. The whole prayer needs to be set against the background of belief that the end of the world is imminent, and that there will be a time of terrible suffering and chaos before the Last Day. Our Lord is not asking that God's name be kept holy (however admirable an idea that is), but rather calling on his heavenly Father to act, to vindicate his power in the midst of the evils at hand. "Father," Jesus says, "hallow your name." "Glorify your name" is the way St. John expresses this plea in his gospel. We say: O God make speed to save us.

The phrase "Thy kingdom come" is a particularly difficult expression for Americans, with our memories of Stuart tyranny and Hanoverian ineptitude. Nor are we helped by the picture of today's constitutional monarchies, whose rulers have had their claws and wings clipped by parliaments. The phrase has added difficulties in that it does not refer to a kingdom in a spatial or geographical sense. The proper word should be something like "sovereignty." We are therefore nearer the original sense when we say: May your rule come throughout the world, or exercise your sovereignty in the world.

"Give us each day our daily bread" is a notorious textual problem for scholars. No one knows the meaning of the word that is translated by "daily." It is a "hapax legomenon" (I justify this lapse into Greek because the phrase is in the Concise Oxford Dictionary), a word used only once for which there are no parallels. "Daily bread" seems to mean a number of things: our food for tomorrow, so that we will not have to worry, or the bread which is our share in the Messiah's banquet when his reign begins. It seems to mean both the natural food to sustain our bodies and the bread of heaven anticipated in the Eucharist.

When we come to the words "Forgive us our sins," we immediately think, "as we forgive those who sin against us." It sounds like a grand bargain with God, a *quid pro quo*. If you forgive me, Lord, I will forgive others, or as some have suggested: Forgive me to the same degree which I forgive others. These interpretations also miss the point. God's gift of forgiveness has no strings attached; it is not a bargain. Rather, the problem comes at our end. We cannot receive his forgiveness if we do not forgive others. Only a forgiving heart can receive and experience forgiveness.

The Lord's Prayer concludes, "Lead us not into temptation," a peculiar phrase which can be quite misleading. Even the ancients were troubled by it, and the Epistle of St. James explicitly denies that God tempts us. One of the attempts to translate the phrase, put forth by the International Consultation on English Texts,

suggests "Do not bring us to the test"—the prayer of every student
everywhere. When it was used in the Green Book for trial use, it
did not last long. Nevertheless this attempt was on the right track.
Life at the end of the ages, with chaos, strife, wars, and devasta-
tion, would certainly be a time of severe testing, in which there
would be a strong temptation to deny Christ and to repudiate our
beliefs, to commit apostasy and save our own necks. The writers
of the Dead Sea Scrolls had the same fear of apostasy under
duress, and in their strange works we find, "Do not let us yield in
the Great Time of Trial." The prayer of the Lord ends on this
urgent note.

The whole prayer, as we find it in St. Luke's gospel, seems
truncated and strange, far from the words that are so familiar, and
far from the interpretations that we have taken for granted. The
discovery of this terse and abrupt form of the prayer does not
mean that we must abandon either St. Matthew's version or the
layers of meaning added through the centuries. The Holy Spirit
has been guiding the church to discover new insights and to find
new meanings. Indeed, the prayer should be so much a part of our
folk heritage that it lends itself to gentle humor. It should be so
much a part of our heritage that it lurks in the recesses of our
minds, as it did in the mind of Edwin Muir.

Still, we do need, from time to time, to look at this ancient
version from the pen of St. Luke. It reminds us of other aspects
of Jesus' teaching which had sometimes been neglected:

   a relationship with God so intimate that we can scarcely
       put it into English,
   belief in a God who has acted and will act to bring about
       his rule,
   knowledge that God wants all his people freed from anxiety
       about necessities and that he feeds us *now* with the
       bread of heaven,
   the vision of a God who forgives unconditionally, but

whose forgiveness can only be appropriated by those
who forgive others,
and the conviction that God seeks our faithfulness in the
midst of troubles as our response to His love.

Robert Greenfield, SSJE

SILENCE, RESISTANCE, AND THE WORD

To write a sermon on the second floor of the monastery is a foolhardy enterprise because of the existence of two telephones, one in the broom closet, the other in a booth at the other end of the hall. Again and again they ring—one man darts to the booth, the other to the closet. After several calls a battle of nerves is engaged; no one answers. The ringing continues; curses resound through the walls and four or five of us burst forth simultaneously. All concentration is shattered. I recall the words of Fr. Benson in a letter written from Boston on January 8th, 1880: "The telephone seems to be a fresh instrument of power getting ready for the centralizing tyranny of Antichrist over the world."

It is quite a remarkable statement, made less than four years after Alexander Graham Bell patented his prototype and only two years after he admitted that the concept of central exchanges linking cities seemed utopian. If the handful of phones then working in Boston seemed like toys, Fr. Benson saw instantly that the advent of the electronic communications media provided the indispensable basis for the ultimate totalitarian control. 'Centralizing tyranny' is not a bad term for the world depicted in Orwell's novel *1984*. As for us, it hardly matters now what further technological progress is made in the media, in techniques of espionage and surveillance, in computerized information storage and retrieval, in methods of mass indoctrination—all the means of absolute totalitarian control already exist.

We don't hear many allusions to Antichrist these days, and yet it is sheer censorship of the Scriptures to pretend to be alert for the coming of Christ while failing to be on the look-out for the Antichrist. In the apocalyptic visions of the New Testament the divine society is preceded by a perverted imitation of it, and the coming Savior is anticipated by rulers purporting to save the people within the embrace of their political system. The New Testament is full of exhortations to *watch*, to be on the alert, to be cool and determined in discriminating between the bogus and the real, the oppressive and the liberating, between Satan masquerading as an angel of light and the Prince of Peace. And this discrimination is presented as something intensely demanding, a test we are to pray to be spared. But it rather looks as though we are not going to be spared. In the season of Advent we ought to look again and see how in the book of Daniel, the book of Revelation, the Epistles to the Thessalonians, and the thirteenth chapter of Mark the believing community is called to *be the resistance* in a world in which the bonds of complex tyrannies are being tightened.

And this is the context where discussion of spirituality belongs in our day. Talk about spiritual life rings pretty false much of the time; a lot of it suggests a past, settled age when the individual cultivated an interior piety and developed the life of the soul by practices of devotion and mortification. The Dewey Decimal Library Classification lumps everything on the ascetical and spiritual life under 240—Devotional Theology—"Experience of quiet confidence in communion with God"! It has a definite escapist ring to it.

For us, spiritual life must be concerned with the grace to live in nonconformity. "Do not be conformed to this age, but be transformed by the renewal of your mind" (Rom. 12:2). For us spiritual life must be concerned with freedom, our own and that of others, from illusion, false values, and the lies and oppression and alienation which penetrate every corner of our society and our world. To live for the Kingdom, to fight for human ways of living, to be the resistance. Asceticism must involve the personal struggle to embody freedom, so we are not just theorizing about it. It must be about not needing to drug ourselves, about sharpening the clarity with which we discern what is actually going on around us, what stems from the principalities and powers and world rulers of this darkness and needs to be named and resisted.

Now what I was actually writing a sermon about when the phone rang was 'silence.' This subject too belongs within the call to be the resistance to Antichrist. For the sheer noise of our western world, the repressive elimination of silence, is a sign of his oppressive power. The theme is one of those running through an amazingly original book, *The World of Silence*, written in the thirties by a remarkable Swiss philosopher, a Jewish convert to Christianity named Max Picard. Sometimes his tone is ironic, where he concedes "there is still perhaps a little silence; a little is still tolerated. Just as the almost completely exterminated Indians are allowed a little living space in their miserable reservations, so silence is sometimes allowed a chink of space in the sanatoria between two and three in the afternoon . . . it is true that silence still exists as true silence in monastic communities. In the middle ages the silence of the monks was still connected with the silence of other men outside the monastery. Today the silence in the monasteries is isolated; it lives literally only in monastic seclusion." (And as we on the second floor know, even that is unsure, now.)

But Picard speaks more directly when he comes to the numbing effect on human responsibility of the mass media, and his words are doubly relevant since the rise of television and the invention of the transistor. "It seems to me that this is the cause of many modern psychoses: an unlimited mass of words is thrown into us through the radio, words that really demand an answer. But there are too many words for an answer to be possible, and no answer is even expected, for at every moment a new mass of words is thrown out. People who still know, somehow or other, that an answer must be given to everything that is brought before the human mind become confused. They feel that an answer ought to be given but that there is no time and no room in which it can be given, and out of this confusion of mind a psychosis can very easily develop that may show itself in all kinds of inhibitions. Such a psychosis may serve as an escape from a world that has taken the most essential thing in life from human beings—our power to answer and to be responsible."

The incessant verbal noise of the media creates a steady stream of propaganda in which we are pathetically vulnerable to the ideologies it is conveying: "Everything therefore is carried along in the noise, and any and everything can develop of it. Nothing arises any longer from a specific act, through a decision and through the creative. Everything turns up automatically; through a kind of mimicry the noise produces what is required by the circumstances of the moment, and this is conveyed to man.

"For example, if the surrounding world is Nazi then Nazi ideas are conveyed by the noise, and this takes place without man's having decided for Nazidom by a special act of his own conscience. Man is so much a part of the verbal noise going on all around him that he does not notice what is being conveyed to him."

In chapter after chapter Picard analyses the damage inflicted on the human psyche when, without spiritual resources of silence, it is bombarded in our western culture with more stimuli and more objects than it can assimilate. "When too many objects crowd in upon him and he has within no silent substance into which a part at least of the multitude of objects can disappear, the resources of imagination and passion which he has at his disposal are insufficient to meet and respond to all the objects. To save man from this invasion and congestion of too many objects that are beyond his power of assimilation, he must be brought into relationship again with the world of silence."

Silence matters to us in our Christian lives and we ought to weave silence into life's rhythm as a resource for healing, psychic rest and assimilation. It is also an element in our critical stance with regard to the world, a means of grace in the refusal to be indoctrinated and manipulated. But as there are many other reasons that would take us along many routes of exploration, let me conclude by mentioning two.

Ours is an age in which language itself is threatened. Words spawn and proliferate like mad, but they have become desperately threadbare and hollow, and prostituted by the lies of human beings and demagogues. The most precious and serious areas of human concern are buried under an avalanche of psychobabble and nonsense. In the Church we sense that words are losing their effect. Words like "grace" and "salvation" give us sometimes a heartbreaking sense of staleness; the air around them has been breathed so long it becomes stifling. It matters to us that words recover their power to be God's word; they can only do so where silence is loved. "In silence," writes Picard, "language holds its breath and fills its lungs with pure and original air. Even when language remains the same, it is able to appear as something original and new as it emerges from silence." St. Ignatius of Antioch spoke of Christ as "God's word issuing forth from silence." And in one of the great antiphons of Christmastide we sing, "While all things were in quiet silence and the night was in the midst of her course, thine Almighty Word, O Lord, leapt down from thy royal throne." We take these as the watchwords of monastic preaching and meditation, but all will need some silence if in the maelstrom and cacophony of the commercial Yuletide we are to hear God's word.

Finally, silence is the companion of solitude and both take us out of the collective. God's word comes to the Church, to a community and a fellowship, but it also comes to us uniquely as individuals. "I love private languages," writes Monica Furlong. "Real intimacy has only been achieved between human beings when they get to the point of talking mostly in code." In silence we learn the particular language in which God speak to us as unique persons.

Martin Smith, SSJE

PRAYER AND SIN

THE MYSTERY OF SIN

I think most of you know that Martin Smith and I act as spiritual directors and confessors to the Episcopal Divinity School community. Each year at orientation one of us speaks to the new students about why we are at EDS, and this year the job fell to Martin. He began his talk by saying, "Now one of the things you will get involved in during this year is a lot of sinning." They all laughed, too. But, as Martin went on to say, before long most students find themselves entangled in complicated relationships involving selfishness, self-delusion, deceit, sexual gratification, and not so carefully disguised hatred. The agony of situations like these might well, he said, be brought to sacramental confession for repentance, comfort, forgiveness, and restoration.

Well, we have all been given this invitation before. The invitation is extended through pamphlets found in shadowy church vestibules, in emotionally wrought counselling sessions, through certain kinds of spiritual reading, and probably in far too many sermons.

'Come,' the invitation says, 'be released from the nagging guilt you feel. Come, be restored in your relationship with God and begin again with those you have hurt. Come, receive God's free gift of forgiveness. Come, feast on the Lord's mercy and love.'

Most of us accept the invitation, sooner or later, in one form or another, and we go to repent of our sinfulness. And all the enticement of the invitation is true. There are tremendously powerful emotions stirred within us through that first absolution. At first we feel a kind of relief we have never felt before, a generosity towards others, and a wholeness in ourselves. We know of God's goodness and his love of us in a way we have never experienced before and in spite of everything we have confessed. We see with such clarity how we offended God and our neighbor.

And we wonder how the situation could have seemed so muddied and grey at the time. "Why did I ever do that?" we say to ourselves. So most of all, after this first experience of repentance and forgiveness, partly because of our gratitude to God but mostly because of renewed faith in ourselves, we are resolute, determined not to sin again, or at least not to commit the same sins as before.

This first experience really is a kind of feast, and the Holy Spirit, whether you look back on it or forward to it, really does hand over everything promised in the initial invitation. But don't think for a moment that the work of creation stops here, that this is as "new" as you will ever be. The process of redemption has not been fulfilled until you *next* feel the need to repent and receive forgiveness, the need for a replenishment every time the tank runs dry. No, the Spirit is calling us on, inviting us to enter fully into the mystery of sin.

From here on, it seems pretty straightforward to me. I know that I will sin again; in my heart, if not in my head, I know that I am already on my way. In thinking it over I see in myself perhaps five important sins which separate me from God and from my neighbor, which hinder me and blur my full humanity.

There is my jealousy. And especially my jealousy of *him*. There is my desire to control that person. To use them physically and emotionally for my gratification. There is my hating of *her*, my persistent judging of other people. There is the laziness in my work, especially the part of the work that is so clearly what God wants me to do and what I like to do the least. There is my inattentiveness at prayer or my failure to bother with it at all.

And so I take these five major areas, so clearly defined, and I set them up like sand towers in a row on the beach, and I wait for God's good grace and my sincere efforts to wash them away. Usually these five sins do wash away, not because of grace or effort, but because of my boredom with them.

But the Holy Spirit is calling me on, inviting me deeper into the mystery of sin, to that realm where the Spirit unveils for me, tediously, carefully, how much I depend on myself. He shows me how thorough is my self-sufficiency.

As I examine myself in this particular realm, after the initial stirring of the emotions, after the firm resolution not to sin again, I look around me to where the Spirit has led me and I see one isolated act against God after another. I see stretching endlessly out before me a kind of list which repeats itself month after month and year after year. The enticement of the invitation fades away and I wonder if I have somehow been misled by another spirit. I repent, but this list of sins could just as easily be the one before this, or even the one before that, and the only thing that stops me from adding to the list is lack of time and my confessor's warning against scrupulosity.

I try to recapture the initial determination. I chip away at one particular sin, and realistically I pick a fairly easy one. But I become discouraged because even with this insignificant sin there is so little progress and when I look around at the rest of myself there is so much more. Examination and repentance in this realm seem to be a hollow duty, and I quite unnecessarily add to the list my *accidie*.

But through all of this the Spirit is calling me on. Through all this tedium, doubt, self-accusation, and failure the Spirit is calling me and I penetrate, without realizing it, more deeply the mystery of sin. It is true, what I've always heard: I do not have the strength to reform my life. There is not enough resolution in me to stop sinning. There is not enough strength in me to avoid even one particular and easily-defeated sin.

In this realm the Holy Spirit shows me that my sin is not so much an isolated act against God or my neighbor, but my participation in the sin of the whole world. The Spirit shows me sin's great power in the world. How strong it is. How it permeates everywhere. How unavoidable it is, even for me. What a formidable adversary it is, never to be defeated by my feeble human will. Here the Spirit connects for me my sins of hatred, suspicion, and desire to dominate with the sins of whole warring nations and histories. Here the Spirit connects for me my greed and self-gratification with the oppressive poverty and misery created by one class's selfishness imposed at the expense of another. I see how I am a microcosm of the world's sin, and how I both feed and am fed by it.

This, I am told, is the realm in the mystery of sin where I will begin to lose my self-righteousness. In this realm to which the Spirit has led me, I will begin to see how totally and absolutely dependent I am on God's grace. The Spirit has led me through the realm of those first emotions, through to the realm of self-improvement, to the tedious, frustrating realm where nothing ever seems to change, to that realm where I will see how completely the world's redemption belongs to him. I think here, in this realm, is where I get the first real glimpse of my humanity and God's divinity. Here I will know that my job is not so much to get better but rather the discovery of where I am to look for my salvation.

The Spirit tells me that here, in this realm, sin becomes almost a friend of mine. This the realm where we come to know most truly the meaning of God's mercy. And it is here that we will know we are winning.

I think it is from this realm, from the mystery of sin, that Dame Julian of Norwich could write the twenty-seventh chapter of her *Revelations of Divine Love*: "And after this," she writes, "our Lord brought to my mind the longing that I had for him before, and I saw that nothing hindered me but sin, and I saw that this is true of us all in general, and it seemed to me that if there had been no sin, we should all have been pure and as like our Lord as he created us. And so in my folly before this time I often wondered why, through the great wisdom of God, the beginning of sin was not prevented. For then it seemed to me that all would have been well.

"The impulse to think this was greatly to be shunned; and nevertheless I mourned and sorrowed on this account, unreasonably, lacking discretion. But Jesus, who in this vision informed me about everything needful to me, answered with these words and said: Sin is necessary, but all will be well, and all will be well, and every kind of thing will be well.

"And in these same words I saw hidden in God an exalted and wonderful mystery, which he will make plain and we shall know in heaven. In this knowledge we shall truly see the cause why he allowed sin to come, and in this sight we shall rejoice forever."

From this realm, the mystery of sin, Dame Julian could see that sin had no being at all. She saw right through its nothingness to the pain it causes and how this pain is for her, and for us, the means of our purgation. She identifies the pain of her sin with that of Christ's cross, and so her sin becomes the way for her and for us to our redemption.

It is from this realm in the mystery of sin that Berdyayev can write that we must go through all the testing of possibilities, we must go through the experience of the knowledge of good and evil, and evil itself may become a dialectic moment of good. Evil and sin can be a dialectic moment in the unfolding development of created things, including that of our humanity, only because through sin the good that is opposed to it is disclosed. First we must live and know and feel our humanity, our createdness, if ever we are to see and know the divinity of God. Sin, in this realm, is almost a friend; when it is accepted and seen in the clear light of God, we can choose the good.

But now a word of caution, a word of spiritual direction. The intellectual apprehension of Julian's showings doesn't make it yours or mine to play with. We cannot skip from the first power-fully felt emotions to the knowledge that sin is necessary but all will be well, and all will be well and every kind of thing will be well. You cannot truly know the power of this world's sin until you know its power in yourself. This showing is God's revelation to Julian, and only meant for our edification. It is a divine entice-ment held out in God's hand to tempt us on further into the mystery of sin and redemption.

We can come to this realm only through the power of the Holy Spirit working within each one of us, as we are. For a very few, that journey may take less than a minute. But for most of us it is a slow unfolding, meant to match the peculiar temperament of each one of us. We cannot rush it, we cannot borrow it from someone else, we cannot produce it of ourselves. All I can do and all you can do is to follow the Holy Spirit as it beckons us through the self-delusion and the tediousness until at last we come into the realm of God's full love and mercy. Until finally we know that here is hidden in God an exalted and wonderful mystery, which he will make plain and we shall know in heaven.

That is the invitation the Church offers to you in repentance and in the sacrament of reconciliation. Come, says the invitation, into the mystery of sin and grace.

Thomas Shaw, SSJE

SO YOU WANT TO GET RID OF SIN, DO YOU?

The French novelist Julien Green was born of American parents who had emigrated after the defeat of the South in the Civil War. I wonder whether anyone here has ever read his journals. All sorts of odd and thought-provoking questions from these journals remain in my mind, as well as these two sharp sentences—

'Je veux chasser le peché de chez moi,' dit le chrétien. 'C'est ça,' fait l'orgeuil, 'je vais t'y aider. Comme ça nous serons tranquilles.'

'I want to get rid of sin from my life,' says the Christian. 'That's right,' says Pride, 'and I'm going to help you. That way things will be peaceful for both of us.'

Once read, that kind of insight remains like a barb in the brain which from time to time will prick us into awareness that our moods of moral fervor and desire to be good are not always what they seem to be. They can be the most dangerous of temptations. Deep down, pride may be reaching out after an illusory condition of superiority and invulnerability. Wouldn't it be wonderful never to need to ask for anyone's forgiveness? Wouldn't it be good not to trip up? Wouldn't it be gratifying to be admired as a good man or woman while having, of course, the humility to take it all in one's stride? Wouldn't it be good (of course, we can hardly allow this to become fully conscious) to be better than others? Purely in order to be of help, you understand.

Corruptio optimi pessima, the Latin tag goes, "the worst thing is the best gone bad." Jesus was fiercely conscious of the demonic possibilities in the desire to be perfect. That is the explanation of his unrelenting criticism of the Pharisees, most of whom were devout people of passionate moral seriousness. The religious life is a dangerous business; it has been said that inside every religious vocation is a can of worms. One particularly slippery one at the bottom is the craving to be, spiritually speaking, above the crowd.

It makes you wonder whether God, most of the time, simply refuses to take the risk of giving us holiness on these terms—perhaps it's better for the Kingdom of God that most of us keep on tripping up than that we should settle down in peace with our helpful partner, pride, after sin has been put out of the door.

Perhaps it would be useful to play with this idea that crops up constantly in the writings of spiritual teachers, and to ask these questions.—Is there a pattern of divine training to be discerned in our ongoing struggle with sin? Is there moral and spiritual meaning behind the fact that we go on being susceptible to sin? Can grace exploit our persistent frailties to bring about that dependence on him which God so prizes?

The first thing we find is that there is precious little warrant in the tradition for the notion that perfection is a condition of achieved invulnerability, a safe state of not sinning. As in the gospels, perfection consists rather in humility and compassion for others. "He who sees himself as he is and has seen his sin is greater than the one who raises the dead" is a typical saying of St. Isaac the Syrian. Another saying has it, "Purity of heart is love for those who fall." So we can start off by saying that God, in refusing to wave a magic wand to make us perfect overnight and in leaving us in our susceptibility to faults and failings, is putting us into a school of humility and patience. We are so keen to correct and improve others, so sure that they could be better if only they pulled themselves together. Well, then, we are left to experience in our own case just how hard it is to change and grow. In order that we may learn to be patient with ourselves, God withholds any artificial protection or premature changes that would disguise our common human neediness and moral poverty. He forces us to recognize, in Jung's words "that the least among them all, the poorest of all the beggars, the most impudent of all the offenders, the very enemy himself, that these are within me and that I myself am the enemy who must be loved." When at length we gain the maturity of that acceptance and are enabled to share it with others, then maybe the path is clear for God in his own good time to clear up some of our besetting sins.

Mention of God's 'own good time' raises the other aspect of the word 'patience,' its temporal aspect. God must not know whether to laugh or cry over the naiveté and impatience which underlies the new convert's surprise that old sins aren't weeded out in a month, that all sorts of objectionable struggles and backslidings appear on the scene in no time. The work of conversion is a process of organic growth, not a conjuring trick. St. Paul speaks of *Christ* being formed in us. This formation has as many stages as Christ's own formation in Mary's womb and through his thirty years in Nazareth. We have stages to go through, experiences to undergo, sufferings to pass through before certain wounds can be healed or habits outgrown. Significant amongst these converting experiences are our personal relationships; we need others to help us grow and change. Perhaps years have to pass before providence brings us into contact with someone through whose example and love God can heal us of some defect. We must take our time—that is the burden of countless classic spiritual counsels. Or, rather, we must learn that God takes his time, that his action in our lives has its own pace and cadence and that his priorities may be radically different from ours. It takes most of us an awfully long time before we begin to get the message.

Now let's consider resilience. According to the great spiritual teachers, our repeated falls can actually be instrumental in deepening and cementing our relationship with God. An enormous amount hangs on how we react to falling. We can either become cynical and discouraged, or we can rage at ourselves, picking off the scabs in regret and nursing feelings of shame and hurt pride in self-prolonging attacks of guilt. This latter reaction is unanimously regarded as a triumph for the evil one and far more destructive than the sinning itself. "Fear," writes Fr. de Caussade, "especially if carried to excess after whatever fault you have committed, proceeds from the devil. Instead of giving in to this dangerous illusion, use every effort to repulse it and cast uneasiness away as you would cast a stone into the sea and never dwell upon it voluntarily. This applies equally to that feeling of uneasiness and distress which proceeds from constant little infidelities. This oppression of the heart is also occasioned by the devil." Instead, the saints teach us a daring elasticity, a loving resilience, which keeps us getting to our feet again and setting our sights on the will of God; it keeps us rededicating ourselves in trust and renewed dependence over and over again. This is beautifully put by Lorenzo Scupoli in his *Spiritual Combat*:

"Every time you fall into some pardonable transgression, even if it happens a thousand times a day, as soon as you notice it, do not torture yourself and so waste your time without profit, but at once humble yourself and, conscious of your weakness, turn to God with hope and call to Him from the depths of your heart, 'O Lord, my God! I have done this because I am what I am and so nothing can be expected of me but such transgressions or even worse, if Thy grace does not help me and I am left to myself alone. I grieve over what I have done, especially as I have no righteousness responding to Thy care of me, but I continue to fall and to fall. Forgive me and give me the strength not to offend Thee again . . . For I zealously wish to work for Thee, to please Thee and be obedient to Thee in all things.' Having done this do not torment yourself with thoughts as to whether God has forgiven you. The Lord is near and listens to the sighings of His servants. So calm yourself in this certainty . . . and continue your usual occupations as though nothing had happened. You must do this, not once, but if necessary, a hundred times and every minute, and the last time with the same perfect trust and daring toward God as the first."

Finally, consider how important it is for God to make sure that many of our best-meant efforts to reform ourselves by resolutions, will power, and good intentions come to nothing, and how much many of us need disillusioning in this regard. We want to do it ourselves. We want control. Actually God doesn't have to do very much for these illusions to come to nothing, except to step aside. Most of our own self-conscious efforts to do better are futile because they are superficial treatments of symptoms, not causes. St. Paul has a phrase, which is 'the mystery of iniquity.' Iniquity is a baffling mystery on a cosmic scale—how did evil arise? And it is a mystery deep in each one of us—the reason why we do what we do—only fully known by God. But it is almost useless to try and suppress the external symptoms if the deep interior causes are not faced and explored.

Beneath the upper levels of psychological cause and effect, our faith holds that at root sins are gambits, substitutes, games and compensations, a thousand manifestations of an unsatisfied hunger for the living God. We lack God, so we treat ourselves as our creator or make others our gods, and the result is myriad destructive games. We lack the all-surpassing divine love that is Father, Son, and Holy Spirit, which alone can meet our craving, so we clutch at ersatz satisfactions and try to wring from others and the world what their creator alone can give. Only sinking into God can change us from within, and this means that conversion, far from consisting chiefly in self-control, is essentially self-surrender, self-abandonment, and worship. The changes that no resolutions of the ego can achieve take place secretly, behind our backs and in the hidden springs of the heart, while we are learning to look to God and finding out that it is safe to trust him absolutely with our life in Christ Jesus.

Martin Smith, SSJE

PRAYER AND DESIRE

ASKING THE QUESTION

"For he was teaching his disciples, saying to them, 'The Son of man will be delivered into the hands of men, and they will kill him; and when he is killed, after three days he will rise.' But they did not understand the saying, and they were afraid to ask him" (Mk. 9: 31-32).

Since I had someone I love very much come about as close to dying as one can come a year or so ago, I can well understand why the disciples of our Lord were afraid to ask him anything more after he told them about his coming death.

I know the gospel text for this evening is a complicated one. But if we can strip away what we know about this passage from Mark—the meaning of the term 'Son of man' in this gospel, the role the disciples and their lack of knowledge play in Mark, the placement of Jesus's prophecies concerning his death—we meet simply a group of men and women who have been terribly attracted to this man. He has come upon them in whatever they were doing, as housewives, fishermen, or tax collectors, and through the sheer force of his personality, his integrity, his teaching, his faith, they have been powerfully drawn to him. How else can we explain it? They are all in love with Jesus. Unless their experience of encountering Jesus is very different than our own experience of Jesus' personality, they probably have never felt so cared for, so understood, so challenged, and so valuable.

And then he tells them that he is going to die. He also tells them he is going to rise again. But I doubt if they could focus on that any more than we believing Christians can focus on everlasting life when someone we love, a parent, a friend, a husband, or a wife tells us, "I have cancer and they say there isn't much they can do for me."

So in spite of the other things this gospel is telling us, it also speaks powerfully to that desire in us *not to know*, that fear

44

which numbs our natural curiosity. Why would the disciples want
to know? Why shouldn't they be afraid to ask questions about an
event which is going to take away from them Jesus, the one who
has loved them and cared for them as nobody else ever has? I
would be afraid. I wouldn't want to know.

That is what I want to preach about this evening—our fear of
asking Jesus questions, and our desire not to understand the mind
of God. For it seems to me that the fear we disciples have of asking questions of Jesus is something our Lord speaks to quite
directly in the gospel. For he is always telling his disciples to ask:

"Ask and it will be given to you."

"If two of you on earth agree, ask anything at all."

"Whatever you ask in my name I will do."

Over and over again Jesus says to them, in every conceivable
situation, "Ask, for heaven's sake, just ask." For early on in his
ministry Jesus picked up on this inability of theirs to form questions, and early on he decided that if they were going to be men
and women of faith, he had better start teaching them to ask some
questions of their own, including some hard ones. If they didn't
start asking questions, then their faith was not going to mature
and survive.

Jesus even tries to get them into the habit of asking questions
by asking them a few of his own.

"Who do men say that I am?"

"But who do you say that I am?"

"What do you want me to do for you?"

"I ask you, is it against the law on the Sabbath to do good,
or to do evil; to save life, or to destroy it?"

Questions. Questions. Questions.

I don't think that the life of faith is any different for Jesus' disciples today than it was for his contemporaries during his lifetime, and I don't think Jesus speaks to us any differently than he did to those disciples. The Word, after all, is timeless and eternal. It speaks truth.

For as I examine my own relationship with Jesus, and as I listen to other people talk about their relationships with him, there is a common thread which runs right from these conversations back through Martha, Mary Magadelene, Peter, James, and John. It goes something like this.

"Well," we say, when we are asked why we don't ask, "I never thought of just asking."
"Never thought of asking?" is the reply.
"Well, I guess I didn't think it would be right to ask," we answer.
"Not right?" comes the question.
"Well," and then there is a long pause, "I guess when you get right down to it I am afraid to ask because I am afraid of the answer."

With that answer, then, there we are, standing right alongside the disciples. Right next to them. And from that position Jesus can do something. For when we have given words to that fear, when we have been able to blurt out, "I am afraid to ask because I am afraid of the answer," we have gotten to rock bottom. And that bottom is a real breeding ground for faith.

Our fear of asking is a seed bed for Christian growth. Our fear is almost a sure sign that we are true disciples of the Lord. It is a sure sign that Jesus, just as he did with Peter, John, and Mary, has called us, and we belong to him. The Pharisees and Sadducees, you notice, didn't have to be taught to ask questions. They badgered Jesus right from the start. The only time the New Testament records that they dared not ask any more questions were in those rare moments of vulnerability, when they could not escape the divine power in Jesus' words and they were struck dumb. It's about as close to faith in Jesus as they ever got.

Acknowledging that fear of asking is the beginning of the kingdom of Heaven.

For that primitive fear of asking questions is a stirring of our faith. We know deep inside of ourselves that Jesus can answer us. We know what Jesus can do. By the ninth chapter of Mark's gospel, the disciples are beginning to get the picture. They knew Jesus was bucking authority, breaking the law. They knew this wasn't any ordinary teacher; they knew because of what he could draw from them and because of what they were able to give. That daring combination must have made them realize the possibility of his death. That combination was bound to get him in serious trouble with authority. They were afraid to ask because they had been given enough of the life of faith, enough of Jesus, to know he was right. And if he was right, they had every reason to be afraid. The disciples were made to face a reality that seemed, at that time, to be a nightmare. They were afraid for him, surely, because they loved him, but afraid for themselves, too, for what would become of them and for how they would fare. Afraid that all their dreams of happiness would be dashed.

That is the kind of company we keep. That is at least part of the reason we are afraid to ask. It is not that we don't think of it, or that it might not be right. We are scared. Scared that what Jesus has in mind for us will dash all of our own dreams of happiness and of fulfillment.

For example, maybe you are a woman getting close to thirty, or a little over thirty, desperately wanting a husband, children, and a home, and fearing now that it might not happen to you. For that might not be what Jesus wants for you. Maybe there is no substance to your dream. And so you don't ask.

Perhaps you are young, ambitious, competent at some job or other, and a certain kind of ministry is what you believe you must have in order to be happy. You shy away from asking what the future will hold because somewhere deep inside you a voice says, maybe that is not what God has in mind for you. It might be better for you if you didn't succeed in just that particular way.

Or maybe you are getting old, not terribly old, but old enough to know that death is getting closer to you, and that you are going to have to go through the process of getting to death. You don't want to ask how you will find the presence of Jesus in your aging because along with the answer to the question might come the vision of what it will be like for you to fail in health.

Or you want to be a person who prays, or a good priest, or a faithful lay person, but you are afraid to ask because you might be given the vision of what that will cost. You might be forced to see how becoming that kind of person will actually come about.

But your worst fear isn't a negative answer and it isn't a rejection of what you want for yourself. That is bad enough, but more fearful than that is the possibility that if you ask, there won't be any answer at all. We are forced to ask that question over and over again in our lives.

And all the while the living Word, Jesus, is hammering away at our fear.

> "Ask and it will be given you."
> "Ask me whatever you wish."
>
> "Whatever you ask in my name I will do."

Why is Jesus so insistent? Why does he, in spite of our fears, keep insisting that we continue to ask him?

Because this is the way he forms us. Because it is only through our questions and his responses that we can begin to find out what Jesus has in mind for us. It's only through hammering it out with him that we can find clarity, vision, find out who he is for us and

who we are for him. Only through our questioning him can Jesus
tell us who he is and what he is like. The formation of our
Christian vocation as religious, as ordained people, as lay people,
how we live and how we die, what we do and who we are, takes
place in the context of this questioning. It is the way we are
finally given our vocations. And once we have been given our
true vocations there is nothing, absolutely nothing, to be afraid
of in life.

You know, too, that when we do ask, when we summon all
our courage and put the question to Jesus, his answer always
comes in the company of his loving, tender, gentle word.

"My yoke is easy," he says, "my burden is light."

"Be of good cheer, I have overcome the world."

"So it is with you; you are sad now, but I shall see you
again, and your hearts will be full of joy, and that joy no
one shall take from you."

"Not one of you will be lost."

Thomas Shaw, SSJE

WAITING AND WEAKNESS

In one of the essays in Annie Dillard's new book, *Teaching a Stone to Talk*, she goes for a walk along the creek near her home in Virginia. She meets a small eight-year-old boy who has a curious, formal way of phrasing his conversation. After they have talked awhile about the boy's horse, his new foal, and his dogs, Dillard writes, "Then the boy paused. He looked miserably at his shoe tops and I looked at his brown corduroy cap. Suddenly the cap lifted and the little face said in a rush, *Do you know the Lord as your personal Savior?*

" 'Not only that,' says Annie Dillard, 'I know your Mother.' It all came together. She had asked me the same question.

"Until then I had not connected this land, these horses, and this little boy with the woman in the big house at the top of the hill where I went to ask permission to walk the land about a year ago.

"I rang the bell. The woman was nervous. She was dark, pretty, with the same trembling lashes as the boy. She did not ask me in.

"My explanation of myself confused her, but she gave permission. She did not let me go, she was worried about something else. She worked her hands. I waited on the other side of the screen until she came out with it.

"*Do you know the Lord as your personal Savior?*

"My heart went out to her. No wonder she had been so nervous. She must have to ask this of everyone, absolutely everyone, she meets. That is Christian witness. It makes sense, given its premises. I wanted to make her as happy as possible, reward her courage, *and run*.

"She was stunned that I knew the Lord, and clearly uncertain whether we were referring to the same third party."

That is an appropriate question for us to ask ourselves this evening as we celebrate the feast of St. Paul's conversion to Jesus Christ. *Do I know the Lord as my personal Savior?*

Presumably we could all answer as Dillard did. At least we do respond affirmatively to that question once a year through the screen door of the liturgy in the Easter Vigil, when we reaffirm our baptismal vows. We would have to answer yes because why else would we be so faithful about celebrating the Eucharist together? And why else would we make such frequent, sincere stabs at praying to God through Jesus? For what other reason would we even attempt Christian ministry if we could not, in some sense, say with St. Paul and Dillard, yes. Yes, I know the Lord Jesus as my Savior.

But we can also understand, I think, why, having answered the woman affirmatively, Dillard wanted so badly to run. She wanted to get out of there not just because the question does seem in bad taste, but because of the question which might so obviously follow a yes response. The one which discerns whether or not we are talking about the same third party. That is, what does it mean for you to accept Jesus as your personal Savior?

It is a question that makes us uncomfortable, makes us want to run because the answer so obviously puts our money, as it were, where our mouths are. For if we answer yes—and what that means for me is that I come to life, to my participation in this life, as one who lives in Christ, as his follower, and imitator—we have also, at some level, to give that response with an awful lot of qualifications. Because, of course, we live in a fallen world and we participate quite a bit in that fallenness ourselves. There are times when our moral and ethical responses are not based on whether or not we have accepted Jesus as our Savior. Those are the times we make decisions, and often conscious ones, to choose not out of our love of our Lord, but from self-interest. What we want, what we think we need, or more likely what we are afraid of. If we are going to answer that way then we have to make a lot of qualifications because there are times, long times, when we don't pray, or even want to pray. When we don't, and don't even want to, act like a Christian. Times when we dig in our heels like Elijah or Jonah, or Peter, or Thomas (odd they are mostly men)

and say *enough* is *enough*. That is why some of us are slightly
uneasy about answering yes to the first question, because we know
what's coming with the second and if we have any self-knowledge
at all that is bound to make us queasy. If this were not the case,
why would we put such a silly over-emphasis on discipline coupled
with accepting Jesus as our Savior. (I am all for discipline but not
when it is an idol.) Using it as though it's a kind of proof or test
as to how much we do know Jesus as Lord.

So how do we say yes to that question? And then wait quietly, self-confidently, for the second shoe to drop. That is, *what
does it mean for you to accept Jesus Christ as your personal
Savior?* Fundamentally I think it means the discovery of the
knowledge that we are being led. Like Paul, the deep visceral
recognition that we have been knocked right off our feet, blinded,
and that now we are being taken, led, by the risen Christ. And
that the recognition and acceptance of this action of God in Christ
is not an isolated event in our lives but one which happens, keeps
happening, over and over again, replenishing, nourishing, giving
self-confidence to that initial visceral discovery that we are being
led by our Savior. We are always being knocked down, blinded,
and then taken somewhere new, someplace we wouldn't have
thought possible. As Paul was taken to the very people he was
persecuting and then on to the Gentiles where, as a Pharisee, he
never would have dreamed of being taken by the God of Abraham,
Isaac, and Jacob.

But how do we discover at the deepest levels of our being that
we are being led personally by Jesus Christ? For what if you have
never had the knowledge, except perhaps at an intellectual level?
Or what if it is a knowledge you so desperately want for yourself,
but you keep turning into blind alleys? It always seems to be
something just beyond your grasp, just outside your understanding. What if it comes only in flashes? And I can't answer the
question of how we discover at the deepest level of our being that
we are being led by Jesus Christ because first of all the question is
personal, individual, tailored uniquely for yourself. And second

because it is always God's action, and cannot be contrived or forced or even guaranteed.

But there are ways we can be ready for it. Waiting, responsive, and attentive, like all those wise virgins and servants of the New Testament. There are ways we can be ready with open arms to receive the experience and cherish it and take it to ourselves. At the least we can avoid resisting it, spinning our wheels going no place. There are some clues.

The primary clue is the Incarnation. For that is, in a sense, when God through our Savior Jesus knocked the world off its feet, blinded it and led it towards restoration in a new way, turning the corner to redemption. If we hold up the Incarnation for a minute we can see how God, *at least once*, revealed to the world that it was being led by its Creator. St. Paul says the deep acceptance of that knowledge of being led makes all of creation groan.

To give the knowledge of its redemption, of its being led away from fallenness, what does God do? God goes to the weakest spot God can find. That is where God breaks through with this knowledge. Divinity finds the thinnest, most transparent spot, and comes crashing through with all the force the love of God can muster. And it is not just the weakest place for us, for the world, but the weakest spot for God, too. God chooses the most vulnerable place within himself to break through. The offering of God's only son Jesus. Like a divine Abraham offering the only-begotten on the altar of the cross. The place in creation God loves the most, men and women—us. The only place God has given the gift of free will, the possibility of rejection, the place we are told, which is so much like God. God goes to the place where he is the most vulnerable to defeat. We and God are alike in that where we love most, we are weakest.

And the place the world seems most likely to discover this knowledge and accept it, if it is to accept it at all, is in its weakest place. A weak, dominated country, as Palestine was at that time,

a religion that had become weak with internal strife, oppressed by
the Law. And then to a woman, unmarried, and weak with an
empty womb. That is where God breaks through, in some back-
water manger. Where God comes crashing into our world as a
helpless infant, changing everything, knocking it all down, blinding the world, and then leading it through Jesus the Savior into
the kingdom of God. And God's son, God's glory in this world,
follows in the tradition of his Creator. He always goes to the
poorest, weakest place, too, to sinners, sick people, the not too
intelligent, and to the weakest point of all, death on the cross, so
that we, the world, might discover that we are being led by God
through him in the power of the Spirit. If God's going to come
through anywhere and manifest God's power, if God runs true to
form, it will be at the weakest place in the world, our personal
weakest spots, and the place where God is weakest, where God is
most likely to be defeated.

So the incarnation of God in Jesus Christ provides us with a
clue of where God might break through in our lives, where we
might experience God's power to lead us. A few were there waiting, receptive to that blinding event of the Incarnation when it
came. They knew where to go and they in turn give us a clue.
Where God and the world are weakest. If we are wise virgins and
servants that is where we should be standing with open arms,
too; where we are weakest and where the world seems to have no
strength to help itself.

That means our prayer, our attentiveness to God ought to be
focused mostly on that spot where we are most vulnerable. And
that's the part that is as unique as you are. It will have everything
to do with who you are, how old you are, who has or hasn't
loved you, where you grew up; those million variables that are
you. Right now the weakest place in your life might be something
as obvious as your health, and that is where you should go to pray,
to wait for God to break through and come to you, knock you
down, blind you, and then lead you. Or the thinnest place in your
life might be that you want someone to love you and you are

anxious and unhappy because that hasn't happened. Or it's your vocation, or financial security. Or it might be some personality trait, such as your desire for certainty in life—and instead feeling yourself thrashed around in the ambivalence that seems to surround you. But, wherever it is, go there to the thinnest places in your life. Don't do what we usually try to do—muster will power, cover over, or underestimate. All of that is resistance; holding at arm's length the visceral experience of God's crashing through to your life. Resistance to the knowledge that we are being led.

You will know, in case I need to remind you, when this knowledge is yours. One person I know describes it as making a connection and she writes a short story about it, another person writes poetry, and some people produce nothing but the knowledge of being led by the risen Christ. The knowledge gives them a new courage, a warmer vision of reality. *Like snakes they shed a skin or two.* There may be, there usually is, some long period of waiting, but when it comes, it comes fast. Like a dam bursting, in a great forceful rush. And then we know, for the first time or all over again, deep in ourselves, that our Savior is leading us.

And this tells us, too, something about where we should be witnessing for Jesus in the world; at the thinnest, weakest spots, waiting for the breakthrough of God. We should be staying as close as we can to people's sinfulness, to the poor, to people who are sick and near dying; spots where defeat seems imminent. It's why nuclear disarmament is such a crucial place for Christian witness now. We are almost stretched to the point of transparency in terms of total self-destruction, no matter whose hands the power is in. That is the weakest place for humanity right now and it is our bounden duty as wise virgins and servants to be there, present to the coming of God in Jesus Christ. The only way to peace for the Christian is the way of our Savior Jesus, in weakness, vulnerability, the shedding of self-defense.

In this sense weakness is sacramental, for it brings the Lord to us, like eucharistic bread and wine, like water in baptism. The possibility of conversion is infinite for us as we wait there, ready and poised to accept and cradle within us the deep knowledge that we are being led by the Lord.

Thomas Shaw, SSJE

RIVERS OF LIVING WATER

"Out of his belly shall flow rivers of living water" (John 7: 38)

In the sixth chapter of his gospel St. John has been setting
forth the intensely disturbing teaching of Jesus on the true bread
from heaven, for he himself is that bread and his own flesh is food
which gives to the one who eats it eternal life. All the time there
is in the background the great story of the manna in the wilderness. Now the sign in the wilderness which follows the story of
the manna comes to the fore—the strange and moving image of
the thirst of the wanderers and their anguish and anger, and Moses
striking the rock and the water flowing forth. I do not just *say*
moving; I am always moved by it. The generations who sang of
it in words of fierce awe take me along with them—"Tremble,
O earth, at the presence of the Lord, at the presence of the God of
Jacob. Who turned the hard rock into a standing water and the
flintstone into a springing well." The image speaks of human extremity, thirst, of hardness of heart and of need. It speaks of inexhaustible resources being tapped right there and then in the most
impossible, unlikely, unpromising and unyielding place. The
flint-stone—a springing well!

Choosing his moment at the climax of the Feast of Taber-
nacles in the Temple, Jesus stands up to speak to those who thirst.
His words are not for the full and the fulfilled; he speaks to the
thirsty and empty, and invites them to come to him. Then his
words are as disturbing as those words about eating the flesh of
the Son of man; the water to quench the thirst of the thirsty will
flow from his belly. "Out of his belly shall flow rivers of living
water." Then the evangelist turns to the reader. This well-spring
of living water, he tells us, is the outpoured and outgiven Spirit
of God with which Jesus in his glorification would baptize those
who believed in him.

Now it was the heart of primitive Christian experience that
the new found and new felt presence and gift of the Holy Spirit

was an outcome and overflow of Jesus' exaltation. At the right
hand of God Jesus was now fully Messiah, the Anointed One.
The anointing Spirit was fully his, and from him it spilt over onto
and into the hearts and the fellowship of those who believed in
him. Luke sets this out in a sequence which is second nature
to us because the Church's year is based on it: Pentecost follows
the Ascension. But for John, the lifting up on the cross, the
raising up in the Resurrection, the exaltation of the Ascension, are
all fused together and focused in one burning ray. "I, if I am
lifted up, will draw all men to myself." Jesus, showing his hands
and his side, breathes the Holy Spirit into the disciples on Easter
Day in the upper room. But John even goes further than this in
making the Passion pentecostal. He wants to show that the gift
of the Holy Spirit flows out of the very depth and heart of the
degradation and death of Jesus, out of his self-loss and suffering,
out of his extremity and self-emptying. And so having prepared
us in the strange prophecy of chapter seven, John allows the image
of the stricken rock to stand out at the climax of the crucifixion.

"After this Jesus, knowing that all was now finished, said (to
fulfill the scripture), 'I thirst.' " The note of thirst and need and
emptiness is sounded once again. Then John continues, "When
Jesus had received the vinegar, he said, 'It is finished'; and he
bowed his head and gave up his spirit." *Gave up*. The word is
carefully chosen; it means bestow and hand over. Jesus gives the
Spirit to his mother and to the beloved disciple, who stand
beneath him as he bows his head. Then comes the striking of the
rock, the flowing forth from the belly. "So the soldiers came and
broke the legs of the first and of the other who had been crucified with him; but when they came to Jesus and saw that he was
already dead, they did not break his legs. But one of the soldiers
pierced his side with a spear, and at once there came out blood
and water. He who saw it has borne witness—his testimony is
true, and he knows that he tells the truth—that you also may
believe" (John 19: 28-35).

In this way John shows the Holy Spirit to be the spirit of
Christ in his loving to the end and to the utmost, the spirit of

sacrifice, conflict, and death. It is possible so to misread and mistake the teaching of St. Paul about the Holy Spirit that we associate the Spirit almost exclusively with miracles, charismatic gifts and power, revelations, uplifting joy, thrilling certainties, and exuberant praise. But here the Holy Spirit is shown to be in the guts of the crucified one. The Spirit's sphere and place is the visceral, gut-level center of love in conflict with evil. There the Spirit lives—just where on the surface appears to be only anguished thirst, defeat, nothingness, and death. There the Spirit is given, when that rock is struck, at the most impossible, unlikely, unpromising, and unyielding place. The implications are endless and profound. I leave them to your imagination, or rather to your meditation.

Now let us go back to chapter seven of John's gospel, to Jesus' proclamation in the Temple. There is another side to it equally significant. "If any one thirst, let him come to me and drink. He who believes in me, as the scripture has said, 'Out of his belly shall flow rivers of living water." The remarkable thing is that the Greek is equally open to the idea that the belly is the belly of the believer. "Out of the belly of him who believes in me shall flow rivers of living water." And whenever there are two meanings possible in John, we are nearly always meant to take notice of both of them.

This idea of living water takes us back to the story of Jesus and the Samaritan woman at Jacob's well in chapter four of John's gospel. Again the theme is thirst. Jesus says to the Samaritan woman, "Give me a drink." And the proclamation is made that he, the thirsty one, is actually the one who is able to quench all human thirst and to meet all human need. "If you knew the gift of God and who it is that is saying to you, 'Give me a drink,' you would have asked him, and he would have given you living water. . . . Everyone who drinks of this water will thirst again, but whoever drinks the water that I shall give him will never thirst; the water that I shall give him shall become in him a spring of water welling up to eternal life" (John 4: 10-14).

"Out of his belly shall flow rivers of living water." The prom-
ise is that the Holy Spirit will be not an intermittent visitor occasionally warming the heart, or a vague inspiration occasionally
influencing the mind. No, the Spirit takes up its home at the very
heart of the believer's being, in the deepest core of our person—
unshiftably centered there, profound, hidden, secret, but flowing
and living, overflowing and moving. And part of us wants to protest "Yes, okay, very mystical, this. It is speaking figuratively
about God's presence in the *soul*, the Spirit lives in my 'spirit.' "
But John won't let us get very far in this spiritualizing and
rarifying of the gospel. He deliberately uses language of a con-
cretely physical kind which is almost gross: "Out of his belly shall
flow rivers of living water." The word *koilia*, 'belly,' has nothing
ethereal about it. It means the soft innards, the viscera, the guts,
sometimes the womb and the heart, the inaccessible inner vital
organs. It is a physical, material word telling us we are thoroughly
bodily creatures; the Spirit dwells in us just as we are, real persons
of flesh and blood. This language faces us bluntly with the
terrible humility of God—take it or leave it. The Word was made
flesh; the Spirit lives in you, in your body. Now show me the man
or woman who doesn't, deep down, want to avoid this, who
doesn't instinctively shy away from it. It's too much.

In the closing months of my school days I was researching a
little dissertation, now lodged in a obscure corner of the County
Archives in Worcester, entitled "Therapeutic springs in Worcester-
shire with special reference to the Droitwich brine-baths." I came
across a Victorian account of an unsuccessful attempt to redis-
cover an ancient well near White Ladies' Aston. In the middle
ages it was a place of pilgrimage and healing for those with eye-
disorders, but was forgotten after the Reformation. I cycled off
to the village with a spade strapped to the bicycle and spent hours
searching in the fields around, until the only spot left was a corner
occupied by a sullen group of cows. Cows and I don't get on, but
I eventually got them away by poking then with the spade, revealing a disgusting patch of dung and mud. Covered in flies and filth
I dug for half an hour, and then the spade struck rock. And

before long I was looking down on a platform of dressed stone enclosing the ancient wooden pipe from which the spring water was now welling up.

I found myself looking at it for a long, long time. I felt I was being shown something of the deepest possible significance. What does it mean to look for God? It means not looking for something to happen, or expecting eventually to arrive somewhere. It means recognizing that God is already here, already given, and that he has already inextricably interwined his life and his being with mine. It means not looking round or looking up, but first and foremost looking to the most impossible, unlikely, unpromising, and unyielding place, my own self, person and body, as the place already lived in and hallowed by the Spirit of the living God. The Spirit has been there all along, as this healing spring had been, although covered by mud and stones.

So the harder part of believing for me was to learn a real reverence for myself, a practical reverence for the mystery of the human person, me and you, as capable of this permeation and this indwelling of God. To learn that I could never be wrong, not even when in the most incommunicable loneliness, bafflement or guilt, in turning with respect and reverence for myself, in acknowledging that within me was a love that stayed with me in unwearying patience, and a beauty which nothing could root out. "Out of his belly shall flow rivers of living water." What if I did not feel it? Do I feel the workings of my kidneys, glands, liver? And if the workings of most of my body occur on a level deeper than feeling, shall not this be even more true of the life of God within it?

Secondly, I was being shown what it was to have a life of prayer. Not prayer that projected words and feelings up at a distant God, but giving myself to, and going with, the love which was already there—the Spirit praying within me. Everything has been already given to me; all I have to do is to experience what

I already possess. And I was being shown that my most inarticulate, clumsy, and unsuccessful prayer was full of a great dignity and worth for the Father, since as St. Paul says, "The Spirit helps us in our weakness; for we do not know how to pray as we ought, but the Spirit itself intercedes for us with sighs too deep for words. And he who searches the hearts of men knows what is the mind of the Spirit, because the Spirit intercedes for the saints according to the will of God" (Rom. 8:26-27).

And finally I came to remember, as I returned often in imagination to my discovery of the spring, how the image in Scripture constantly sounds the note of thirsting and desiring. And what indeed does the word 'belly" suggest, but desires and needs and urges and longings? For in this deep, dark core of ourselves are lodged instinctual and sexual, primal subconscious and visceral energies and reactions—very ambivalent, very complex. And does God's pure, holy, and life-giving Spirit dwell *there*? Apparently it does. Apparently the chaotic and the dark and the unformed is the Holy Spirit's special element and home, as when "the earth was without form and void and darkness was upon the face of the deep; and the Spirit of God was moving over the face of the waters."

Shall I not then have to give up my constant attempts to think of God's grace as a supernatural, uncontaminated radiance from above? I shall. I shall have to learn that from below and from within he knows intimately these complex drives, energies, and longings; from below and within he struggles with and uses, and can direct and integrate and consecrate, these very creaturely and fleshly urges. And shall I not have to stop being afraid of that sense of unfulfillment I experience, underlying all my experience and achievement? Yes, I shall. I will have to learn to see this sense of unfulfillment to be at its deepest level my greatest asset, to see that it is really desire, that God-implanted and God-seeking desire spoken of here.

62

"And let him who is thirsty come, let him who desires take the water of life without price" (Rev. 22:17). Just here is where we have to strike the rock.

Martin Smith, SSJE

MOTHERS AND FATHERS

Most of us have a female friend, or it might even be you yourself, whose childhood was a tortuous affair full of fear, cruelty, manipulation, perhaps some physical abuse, and all on account of a father who didn't know how to be a father. He might have been a physically big man, bigger than his daughter and his wife, and he used this strength to tyrannize and exploit his children, especially the female children, and his spouse. He might have been an alcoholic father, subject to uncontrollable fits of rage that would be translated into sudden attacks on his daughter. Or perhaps he was simply an unhappy human being who took out his sense of failure on the little girls of his own household by picking on them, belittling them, and constantly punishing them because they, unlike the world he was angry with, were too small to fight back, and too tiny to protest. Possibly he was a silent and remote father who only rarely, if ever, showed signs of affection, or tenderness, or encouragement to his little girl. Or maybe he was a man who didn't know, or want to know, much about women at all and expected to be waited on and deferred to, but never questioned or challenged.

And now that daughter, the little girl, your female friend, or you yourself, is a woman. She doesn't live at home any more. Her father might be dead. But she cannot forget. Some trivial incident may happen during the day and suddenly it is all there, right below the surface. She remembers how hurt she was when he ignored her and how frightened she was when he came home late at night drunk. How he would humiliate her and even persecute her in front of her brothers and her friends. And so now, years later, when she is walking along the river and trying to pray, or when she comes to church to pray the liturgy, the name "Father" gets stuck in her throat. The words "God our Father" are lost to her. They drown in a multitude of unhappy memories. The prayer will not come.

Again, perhaps, you have a male friend, or it might even be yourself, who thinks of his childhood and his adolescence as a kind of quicksand from which he never thought he would get out. He remembers his mother, who took the feminine activities of nurturing and caring to a dark extreme, where they became possessiveness and then a kind of suffocation that oppressed him. His boyhood memories are full of the guilt she aroused in him, the insidious manipulations, and the expectations she placed on him. Her demands, tears, and her complaints and her constant fussing over him. And now your male friend is a grown man who lives as far away from his mother as he possibly can. But he can't forget, either, how angry he used to be with her, how much she stifled him, how embarrassed he was, and how humiliated he was by his lack of privacy. And so now, for him too, when he hears a sermon about the motherhood of God he cannot bring himself to respond to it. All that he can see is the image of a crippling, maternal relationship, from which it took him years to extricate himself.

Of course it isn't quite that clear cut. Boys also have imperfect fathers, and girls have mothers who don't seem to have much of an idea of what it is to be a mother. But I think you can see what I mean.

Mothers and fathers are on my mind, because today we celebrate the feast of the parents of the Blessed Virgin Mary, the grandparents of our Lord. It is the occasion of this feast of parenthood that has started me thinking about the parenthood of God, of God being both our father and our mother, and how important it is for us not just to think of God in that way, but to *respond* to him in that way too. Far from being an obsolete image, the parenthood of God is essential to our experience of prayer. In the Old Testament and in the New, God is always asking to be called Father, or Daddy. It is an image that God won't seem to let go of, at least according to Scripture. Why is that? Why is it so important to God? And why is it that some spiritual giants, along with some of my contemporary female friends, and occasionally me, seek out the word "mother" for God in our prayer and find that no other word will do? Why is this so frequent, this recurrence of an image of parenthood as a means of finding God and, more importantly, God's way of finding us?

The bottom line, of course, is that the image of parent and child effectively puts us in our place. It describes our situation and defines pretty accurately who we are. We are made. We are creatures. You and I are flesh and finite. We could not exist were it not for the existence of someone else. We had to be brought into being. And we know too, through prayer, that our creation is not a once-and-for-all event. We know we are always being brought into being. We are always being molded and shaped by someone else. Sometimes we try, in one way or another, to claim that we are not creatures, and finite, and made. But we are quickly reminded of this fact, even if it is only through that last obstacle to infinity, death, that proves to us that we are not finite. At the bottom line we are the offspring of our Maker, the creatures of our Creator. Sin tells us that isn't always how we would like it to be, but in our most human moments it is where we are most comforted, and most at peace.

For we know that our Maker is not some cold, unfeeling production-line assembler. We were made from love. We were made and are being made from this crackling, dynamic interchange of care, of giving, of pouring from self to self within the three persons of the Trinity which spills over into the act of our being made. God is not like an entrepreneur who needs to make money in order to be fulfilled. God doesn't need to create us in order to be fulfilled; rather, you and I are the expression of God's fulfillment.

God reveals to us that we are the result of love, the expression of fulfillment within the divine life of the Trinity. God steps into and wades round our humanity and comes up with the most powerful image he can find: parenthood, fatherhood and motherhood. This is the relationship that seems to pinpoint exactly what

we are in relationship to God: creatures, offspring, the conse-
quence of love. It is also how we are meant to relate to and pray
to God. God asks to be called Father.

We know, of course, that there has never been anything either
passive or idealistic about parenthood, now or in the past. It is a
powerful image because of its potential for communicating love;
also, and just as significantly, because of its potential for conveying hate. Surely God has known from the very beginning
about good parents and bad parents, of loving ones and hateful
ones. Any way you look at it, the quality of parenting determines
the life of the child. God is not stupid and the interpreters of
God's will—prophets, priests, and story-tellers—are not stupid,
either. All of them are aware that all parents are not good parents.
In fact, they probably saw even as we do that most fathers and
mothers are not good parents and that even the best are imperfect; yet we are clearly encouraged to call God Father and sometimes Mother. In one sense God puts his final stamp of approval
on this manner of relating to God by coming to us as a son, as
Jesus. The Incarnation tells us this is the unique way of relating
to God in concrete, human terms. And through the Incarnation,
remember, God is always forcing us to be specific and personal
just as he forced himself to become personal and concrete in the
man, Jesus. God only asks of us what he demands from himself.

Why is God so insistent on being called Father? Why is he so
determined to be our parent? Why does God choose this poten-
tially destructive image of alienation and hate in order to draw us
into relationship? Why does God insist, and he does, that my
friend with a couple of decades of mistreatment from her
biological father, nevertheless call God by the same name? Why
does God urge this image on her, when he knows how frustrating
it is for her? And why must my male friend be pushed to experience God as mother?

He does this for some of the reasons I have already given.
These names reveal our relationship and our way of relating to

God in the concrete fleshly terms so necessary for our salvation. At the same time, I think God is so insistent that we call him Father or Mother for our own sake, and for the sake of our healing. He does it in order to reconcile that fragmented, distorted, even destructive experience of parenthood in the past that we have all suffered to some degree. It is another case of God's restoring love. Through our heavenly Father's love we are able to see true fatherhood and true motherhood, true authority and honest concern, instead of the travesty we have so often experienced in the past. When we pray to God and call him Father, or Daddy, or Mother, and presumably Mom, we invite the parenthood of God into the damaged reality of our experiences with biological mothers and fathers. In a very real sense, we are petitioning God for wholeness. We ask the Father to come, make over, and renew what went so wrong. We ask him to restore the child who has been so badly battered—the child who lives now partly through that tarnished image, the one who sees the world slightly or more than slightly askew because of what once happened to her. Now that child desperately wants to break out of the prison of that past.

In asking us to call him Father and Mother, God is offering us a way of being free. We can be free of what has shackled us in those past experiences of being fathered or mothered. Go on, God says to us in prayer, call me Father, so that you and I can break through to the true experience of parents and children. There we are free to be creatures, experiencing that eternal love of our creator and our maker. Finally, we will become free enough for each one of us to forgive our own mothers and fathers for being less than God's image of fatherhood and motherhood, able finally to let them go and have them given back to us in Christ.

PRAYER AND CHANGE

PRAYER AND CHANGE

I have been asked to preach on prayer, taking the life of St. Catherine of Siena as an inspiration and a stimulus. Time is too short to consider the spiritual teaching contained in her letters and writings, but just to consider the shape of her life is enough to set us thinking. From one angle she seems a figure safely remote, with only the barest relevance to your life or mine. She was born in 1347 in Siena. From a very early age she felt an intense call to a life of totally demanding intimacy with Christ. Against terrific pressure from her parents to get married and live an average sort of life, she joined a group of lay people devoted to the gospel and prayer, which was affiliated to the Dominican order. It was so clear that she was a true mystic that people from every walk of life gathered round her to learn from her. She guided hundreds of people. She died burnt up, as it were, by the intensity of her life at the age of thirty-three.

But that is only half the story. The times she lived in were horrifically turbulent and bloody. Italy in particular was racked with warfare between rival cities and states and marauding mercenaries. The Church was in a chaos of corruption, with one unworthy pope after another living in France in utter disregard of their spiritual task. You might think it understandable if Catherine remained in seclusion and concentrated on her relationship with God. But she didn't. She was a powerless girl, utterly devoid of wordly connections and influence and plagued with ill-health. But her passion for Christ's peace compelled her to intervene in the world of politics and the life of the Church; she stuck her neck out in costly, daring, and ceaseless action. Letters demanding repentance and change, which insisted on God's will for peace, streamed from her to generals, kings and queens, bishops and popes. She went on peace missions and actually succeeded in making the pope return to Rome. Many changed in response to her uncanny authority. Others abused her for her interference and many of her hopes met with bitter

failure. Like the Lord she loved she died at thirty-three, aware of
how the poor and the peacemakers are crucified by the rulers of
this world.

Saints are disconcerting people. God uses their lives, as they
exist in our recollection of them, to make us feel uncomfortable
with our safe, conventional views. Modern Christians tend to
think of the life of prayer as a personal, individual matter of
devotion; who thinks of contemplation as having anything to do
with politics and the world of clashing power groups? Yet here
is a saint who was a mystic *and* a peace activist. She and a
thousand other saints tell us that a passion for intimacy with God
and a passion for social justice and peace are inseparable. The
two vocations are both aspects of a single call. They are both
about the power of love to create change.

Prayer changes us. We all know how any real relationship of
depth or intimacy opens us to being changed and affected. We
have to respect the mystery and the otherness of the other person,
and if we do, something of our own mystery is brought to light
and things within us we never knew were there are brought into
play in the give and take of love. We are really challenged and
tested; we either respond to the newness which begins to emerge
or we clamp down on it. Keeping company with God involves
becoming aware of God's feelings; his disturbingly intense care
and love for me; his probing insight into my depths showing up
talents I refuse to acknowledge and use, and as much as I can
take it, the extent of my fear and faithlessness and all that is still
unhealed. In prayer I can rest in his love but he won't let me rest
in my immaturity and fear. He has a passionate creator's care for
my growth.

In prayer we come up against God's holy otherness as a loving
pressure calling us on to what we can become if only we would
let go. But most of us are afraid of the changes that letting go
would involve. "Some of us are genuinely afraid of the dark, but
all of us are afraid of the light." Even if we are in a pretty poor

state, a little voice tells us it's better to play safe and stick with our personal status quo that to be drawn into changes in our identity we hadn't bargained for. Better a bad certainty than a good uncertainty. So we don't have to look any farther for the basic reason why prayer is so shallow and such a low priority for so many professing Christians. God is in the change business. 'If anyone is in Christ there is a new creation'.

But we are threatened by the summons to freedom, to growth, and to new life. If we prayed we would have to hear that summons all the time, and expose ourselves day in and day out to that incomprehensibly rich and disturbing mystery we call the love of God. In prayer the love of God gets right inside us and nothing can then be the same, so that, as the letter to the Ephesians says, "according to the riches of his glory he may grant you to be strengthened with might through his Spirit . . . that Christ may dwell in your hearts through faith; that you, being rooted and grounded in love, may have power to comprehend with all the saints what is the breadth and length and height and depth, and to know the love of Christ which surpasses knowledge, that you may be filled with all the fulness of God" (Eph. 3: 16-18).

Prayer, then, puts us in touch with the feelings of God. But God does not just feel for individuals. God feels for his people, for societies, nations, groups, churches. He is agonized by their sickness, he yearns for their healing, their sanity, their reconciliation, their peace. In prayer the feelings of God, the love, the cares, and the pain of God set our nerves vibrating; those same feelings are reproduced and stimulated in us. This is what it means to be in the image and likeness of God, and it is the secret of the prophets. The prophets were caught up in a personal intimacy with God, but before they knew where they were, their hearts were filled to overflowing with God's feelings about his people. Feelings of sorrow, disappointment, and pain. Feelings of searching love seeking to woo the hard-hearted people back to the covenant. Feelings of hope that there was still a chance to avert the disasters arising from their disobedience if they would

respond and repent. The prophets were compelled by these
vibrating feelings not merely to pray for the people but to speak
out, to act, to get involved, to run risks, to get attention through
holy publicity stunts, anything to gain a hearing for God's call to
justice and peace and a radical change in the whole order of
society so that it should be his kingdom.

The involvement of the prophets made them controversial
and unpopular figures. Jesus, treading the same path, knew his
rejection would be the climax of their prophetic experience, as
well as the inauguration of a new line of disciples and prophets
who would follow the way of the Cross. "Nevertheless I must
go on my way today and tomorrow and the day following; for
it cannot be that a prophet should perish away from Jerusalem.
O Jerusalem, Jerusalem, killing the prophets and stoning those
who are sent to you. How often I would have gathered your
children together as a hen gathers her brood under her wings,
and you would not!" (Lk. 13: 33-4)

What makes Christian prayer Christian is that it draws us
into the life and the way of Christ. In prayer I experience personally and intimately in my own heart God's care for me and
my life, and I expose myself to his active, life-giving, tough,
transforming love. I receive the Holy Spirit, I cry 'Abba', father,
with and in Jesus. But equally and simultaneously I am exposed
to and experience his care for the world, for our society, for the
nations and the community I live in. His passion that things be
different, so changed that they will become his kingdom,
becomes alive in my feelings and in my will. It is a passion that
makes for action, that judges our apathy, goads our indifference
and sends us out to be witnesses to peace and agents for change,
along the way of and in the spirit of Jesus crucified.

Martin Smith, SSJE

MATURING PRAYER

On November 14, 1940 Coventry Cathedral died in flames
during the obliteration bombing which set out to destroy the
entire city. The rebuilt cathedral, dedicated to a vision and
ministry of reconciliation, welcomes light through ten great
windows. These windows, in their color and design, contain
suggestions of the answers to the two great quests which Christians seek to unfold . . . the truth about God and the truth about
human life, and the relationship between the two. The cathedral
is so designed that the composite picture is only to be seen from
the altar, suggesting that only with full membership in the Church,
beginning at the font and through all the instruction and discipline
of the Church, can these truths be fully understood. And only
under the power of God's own Spirit can the truths come into our
lives fully.

The windows are designed in pairs, and each pair traces a portion of the quest of our lives from origin to fulfillment. After
passing from the initial stages of life represented by the portrayal
of new shoots of fresh growing life and the springtime and fertility
of human life in the initial green windows, there is a pair of red
windows which typify God's intervention in human life in the
historic religions of the world and in individual human responses
to God's initiative. The red windows portray struggle and rough
passage so characteristic of young adulthood through physical and
spiritual dangers, questions of identity and self-gift, to a plateau
time of relative tranquility.

From these there follow two sets of windows which character-
ize maturity, and it is here that we first wish to find our place
today. One of the pairs is multi-colored. The other pair is blue
and purple. The multi-colored windows speak of the conflict and
struggle in human life. All kinds of calls for allegiance wearing
every hue and color clamor for our attention and loyalty. These
first windows that speak of maturity speak of a power for evil

which clamors for our allegiance, and they speak of the struggles
we experience living in a world of time and space—our struggles
with materialism, indifference, worldliness, and power. Within
this multi-colored context, our need is for light which clarifies
who we have become and how we choose to live in the time of
our maturity. The windows clearly emphasize that Christian
life is a pilgrimage—that we have not totally arrived at our desti-
nation yet. These bright windows with their chaos of colors call
us to clearly recognize in ourselves both the occurrence of
temptation and the necessity of a struggle if our lives are to be
whole-heartedly Christian. It is easy, almost seductive, for us to
concentrate on the evil around us and within us.

However, we are in the middle of Lent. And in this season we
are called to be on pilgrimage with Jesus. Each day of Lent
invites us to focus on Christ as he chooses in the midst of the conflicts which surround him and which intensify in the days ahead
of us in this season.

What is our position and our need in this multi-colored season
of our lives? .What do the conflicts look like as they clamor for
our attention? Although individuals experience the conflict in
very individual ways, there are common lines we can consider.
The conflict usually touches our desires and ability to love. A
famous retreat master in the midwest is noted for standing eyeball
to eyeball with an unsuspecting member of the congregation
during a retreat address and declaring in the loudest voice I have
ever heard: "After the honeymoon, it's all a lot of hard work,
honey." After our initial reaction of "Phooey on you, buddy"
we can all attest that whatever the particular shape of our Christian lives, after the new green beginnings, love demands a lot of
hard work. One of the clearest ways we experience the conflict
is to wonder whether love is enough. There are attractions to be
someone, to have power, to make our lives secure, to experience
relief, to settle in life with a bit of comfort, and above all to set
limits on how much we will give. After all, articles on burnout
indicate that it is almost epidemic in mid-life. The real battle-

ground for most of us is within our hearts. The great Fathers and Mothers of our Christian church in the patristic and monastic tradition talked about holy warfare. They had a clear sense that our survival as loving Christians was dependent on a victory which must take place first in our hearts and then extend its influence to others in a life for others. In mid-life Teresa of Avila tells her nuns of the reformed Carmelite monastery as they started over:

> It is most important—all-important, indeed—that we should begin well by making an earnest and most determined resolve not to halt until we reach our goal, whatever may come, whatever may happen to us, however hard we may have to labour, whoever may complain of us, whether we reach our goal or die on the road or have no heart to confront the trials which we meet, whether the very world dissolves before us.

Teresa expresses very boldly our challenge: if we are going to give up our lives—die on the way—it is better to die to some purpose. An initial obstacle to be overcome in our thoughts if we are to stay clear-sighted about our goal and the means to our goal is our attitude to this reality: Love is enough, whatever form it takes. Do we really believe we are made for relationship with God and with each other—expressed in sacrificial love? That these two reciprocal dimensions of love and relationship are what would make us happy and fulfilled?

It is with this demanding view of life in mind—that of loving God with our whole heart, mind and body, and our brothers and sisters as ourselves—that the Gospel asks us bluntly: "What good is it to gain the whole world and lose our very selves?"

To continue to live a life totally given to God and to each other is often experienced as a kind of continuous death, a death to our limited perceptions, understanding, private points of view. It is the kind of death we can assent to and even embrace with joy if we understand that the work of our saving is primarily God's work, and God won't fail unless we make it impossible for him to continue to call on us. In this demanding, multi-colored season, we struggle and pray that God be free in our lives. If God is our companion in the struggle, we seek a transformation of our aggressions and our desires. If God is our companion, we seek a way out of the conflicts so we can love. That the transformation of our capacity to love should be maintained and deepened is not possible unless we are growing in an ability to surmount the conflict we meet within our individual selves and the world in which we live. To face all the hardships involved demands courage. To continue to live a loving life demands courage. Love *demands* courage.

There is a second set of Coventry windows which depict maturity, you may recall from my opening sentences. These two windows are blue and purple. One window portrays a mature Christian life of faith in God and loving service for God's people as a flower in full bloom, colored in the colors of peace and still-ness. The windows suggest that peace and stillness are the reward for Christians who are faithful, whose hope is set in the resurrec-tion of Christ and who have gained the courage to believe that death is not the final word about our lives.

The other window speaks of the maturity of suffering borne by Jesus. On Good Friday the liturgy will ask us with startling directness and poignancy: "Look and see whether there is any suffering like my suffering." This window portrays a chalice traced throughout the whole length of the design. The windows depict our deepest possibilities—that our lives, too, might become such an offering. And the window portrays the possibility of our deepest failures—that in refusing to love and to relieve the suffer-ing of others, we become the chalice of pain and agony of Christ in the garden. The choice of how far we will go is our choice in maturity.

We find ourselves in the middle of Lent. The season of mature, suffering, sacrificial love. The purple season.

Will we keep going? How can we keep going? Will we stay with Christ on the pilgrimage all the way? How do we keep from losing heart? Is it really possible that the stillness of the purple flower completely open, in repose, poised on a slender stalk, could be an apt illustration of our lives in maturity? Our lives are still situated between the conflicts portrayed in the multi-colored windows and the chalice which portrays a life of total self-surrender—love without reserve.

How might we move into the weeks ahead in Christ's company? Let us ask God to show us God's face and heart in human flesh—in Jesus who lives without end. Could Jesus be the source of our courage? Could Jesus actually be our courage for every day? A lot of questions crowd up from our hearts to our lips, because one of the characteristics of maturity is to taste death in the midst of every day life. Sometimes the experience is the simple and stunning realization that there is no longer a generation ahead of us in charge. We have become that generation and we, too, will diminish and die.

Let's try to situate ourselves in this season and find our place in Christ. We're asking whether we can entrust our deep yearnings to live, to love without end, and the terrible realization of our inability to do so, to Christ who will go before us, teach us, encourage us, and actually give us the new hearts we need. Let us see what Christ's courage before God makes possible for our own.

The Gospel we heard is from the tenth chapter of St. Mark. What is going on? Jesus and the disciples are on the road. They are going to Jerusalem. Now Jerusalem is the place where prophets die and none of the disciples were totally ignorant of the possible outcome of the storm which had been gathering strength around Jesus. As a matter of fact, as we heard in the lines proclaimed, Jesus took the Twelve aside and began to tell them what was going to happen.

We should look again. What do we see? The disciples were in

a daze and they were apprehensive. I should stop a moment and ask whether there are any dimensions in my life where I am dazed and apprehensive before the challenges of maturity. Maybe I have already found my place.

The passage tells me something else. Jesus goes ahead. He leads the way. Luke tells us that Jesus resolutely took the road for Jerusalem. It was not easy for him. In fact he seemed to feel the cost of not having a secure place to lay his head . . . even the wild animals had that.

It is not easy for Jesus in Mark's gospel, either. We can imagine with what seriousness and earnestness he tried to communicate to the Twelve what was to lie ahead. How much he wished they would understand. And how expensive it was for him—how much he felt their utter incomprehension and resistance to what he said. We blush in embarrassment as we hear James and John wrangle about who will get the first place immediately following this. Right here we could give Jesus a name for the days that lie ahead in our season of maturity. We might address him, call upon him as the one who goes ahead of us and leads us on our way.

This section of the Gospel offers us some more encouragement in the person of Bartimaeus. Even as the Gospel invites us to focus on Jesus in every way so that we, too, might experience him as the true light for our maturity and our source of strength as we follow him all the way to Jerusalem, we are given Bartimaeus, who focuses completely on Jesus in a number of ways . . . . in his cry for pity, in his perseverance, in the gesture of throwing off his cloak, in his faith, in his experience of Jesus' healing power . . . . and in joining Jesus on the way. The pilgrims scold Bartimaeus and demand that he not interrupt the pilgrimage. Really, of what importance is one man's blindness when this preacher is surrounded by a crowd? The lines are a study of contrasts.

This blind man knows he cannot see. And he knows what he wants. He knows what he needs. Upon hearing the prayer, Jesus stops. Jesus is different from the crowd. It is Jesus who becomes present to this man and his needs. It is an encouraging example, showing yet another instance of Jesus being always ready to give people a new start. Jesus always believing in new possibilities. Jesus never breaking the bruised reed. For him no situation is ever hopeless.

As we pause, perhaps our greatest need is to hear the question: "What do you want me to do for you?" What do I want him to do for me? What do you want him to do for you? Sometimes we don't know, and are not nearly as fortunate as Bartimaeus is. It is an important place to be in these coming weeks.

If we don't stop, and let our need for courage and light really touch us in this season of the maturity of suffering love, we will come to the services of Holy Week like voyeurs suddenly thrust into the most intimate moments of a man's life. And we will feel like outsiders. We will have missed the opportunity for companionship that this Gospel offers us. We will be poorer for it. And we will not be ready for Easter.

So I suggest that we pause right now in Lent and ask ourselves: is there a place in my life where I need courage? Is there a place where I am losing heart? Weary? Feeling blind? Resentful that I have to give up so much? Afraid that love will lead to death? Is there any place where I am tasting failure? Am I disillusioned?

We are given the face of Christ, the heart of Christ, in the days ahead and we are invited to contemplate him with great singularity. What is he about? If you glance at the episodes which follow in Mark's gospel, it is clear that there are many places where Jesus faces the kind of human experiences of death that tear us apart. He experiences betrayal, loneliness, the failure of his mission, the challenge to forgive, the tree that bears no fruit, challenge to his authority, questions about where allegiance should go. He faces mockery, pain, humiliation, the distance of the very God he has staked his life upon.

In the days that lie ahead of us, Jesus faces all of the challenges that present themselves to our human hearts. He asks for our companionship, and promises to go ahead of us because he knows we are frightened and in a daze.

With Christ we are called to a suffering love that experiences the failures as well as the successes of self-giving generosity, and with him we are called to approach death with the conviction that it is not the final word. Christ's own courage will be given to us, and new hearts will be given to us, as long as we reach out to anyone and all people who have need of a new heart. Such bigheartedness—often when we feel that our hearts have no more room and no more strength—comes as we increasingly recognize that the sufferings of all the earth are truly our own. Only Christ can teach us this. And only if we love as Christ did.

God calls us through the power of God's Spirit to a radical hope and love in this season of mature love. We are called to a terrible hope that suffering love can redeem us all and draw us to live that way for each other. With the courage of Christ before us as a model and as our way, we seek new ways this day to give our total lives—even our entire lives—for each other. We seek a share in the community of Christ that will make a difference in our world.

In an essay entitled "Color," Janet Erskine Stuart suggests that we see our place and compose ourselves as a ray of sunlight dispersed through a prism into seven bands of monochromatic light. Remarkably she, too, colors our middle, mature years in shades of blues and purples. In the early middle years she would color us blue. . . . . a time of reason. She cautions that the risk of the early middle years is that we may cut and grind down our ideals and those of others. She warns that if wary reason stops and sounds too dubiously the chasms over which our feelings and imaginations must leap in the challenges of the middle years, then our riper and more mature years will be dwarfed. The middle years of our maturity she would color indigo. If our dialectic years have colored our life black, we will have made for ourselves a painted sky and painted stars, but if our middle years have given depth to our blue then we will have reached the age of true asceticism and true discipleship . . . . deep, responsible, austere, keen-eyed, daring in thought and strong in act, greatly illuminated from heaven. And in the true ripeness of middle years, she would color us violet . . . . the last band of monochromatic light, the time when we finally are what we are. She reminds us that this violet light is the most refrangible of all rays, and possesses the greatest ability to let light through. She asks us: "Why are there so few to sing the glories and graces of middle life?"

Ann Goggin, rc

APPROACHING OLD AGE IN THE SPIRIT

I am glad that the title given me for this homily was not being old, but rather approaching old age in the Spirit! All of us are acquainted with some people who are already old in their twenties or thirties, and who seem to have ceased to be alive and growing. It is, however, not of this type of person that I wish to speak today. Rather would I speak of those of us who as "older" Christians are seeking still to be growing into the measure of the stature of the fullness of Christ, and who believe quite literally that our life here on earth is our daily response to God's call to us to follow Him, and so to be led at last into the Kingdom. As Christians, too, we are not following alone, but rather as members of the people of God, gathered into particular relationships and communities. How greatly I rejoice that I am preparing, learning to grow old with all my brethren here, and in particular relationship of love and friendship with many of you who form part of our worshiping and sharing community here.

We can be growing old in the Spirit only as we truly believe that the Holy Spirit is a living spirit who dwells in us, and who is continually reforming and recreating us in that image of God, in which each one of us has been created. We can be growing old in the Spirit, only as we seek to make all of our life our response to God's call. On a very hot, sticky Sunday afternoon in July, 1939, when the gospel for that day had been the account in the fifth chapter of the Gospel of Luke of the call of Peter and Andrew, and James and John, I was admitted here in this chapel as a postulant in our Society. What the Lord said to me then, he has been going on saying every day since: "Put out into deep water. Do not be afraid." Not always have I truly responded; sometimes I have drawn back in fear, or have sought a false security. Thank God that he has always kept on calling me, and still continues to do so.

God is the creator of time, and calls us to live in time and with time. To approach old age, to grow old in the Spirit, it is absolutely essential that we believe that God is revealing himself to us in time. There are, I believe, two special temptations which come to the person who is approaching old age; to yield to either or to both is truly to deny that God is the "I am," the one who is. The first temptation is that of looking backward in an unrealistic, nostalgic, possessive manner to "the good old days"; or, on the other hand, of looking backward and seeing the past as predominantly unsatisfactory or destructive. Because we believe that God has created time and that He continually redeems it, because we are a covenant people and so believe that God works and manifests himself in history, which includes our own individual histories, we look backward in order to be able to live more creatively and realistically in the present. As each one of us looks back on our own life, we seek to discern our individual past in its wholeness, and to see all that has gone before in our lives as a part of the "stuff" of our present life. To grow old in the Spirit involves growing in love of ourselves, recognizing all that was both good and bad, positive and negative in all that has occurred in our lives up to today.

The second temptation is to be fearful about the future, about our growing incapacities, or prolonged illness, and finally our own death. I must admit that I have personally faced a real struggle in myself about my own death. No so much in regard to suffering, but rather because I prize so highly my life in our community, and am so concerned and interested in our future— because of my close bonds of love and friendship—because of the uncertainty of death and of what follows it. Rather a paradox for one who enjoys travel as much as I do!

It was during a community retreat two years ago that I realized that I must seek to come to terms with the fact of my own death. In the time that has elapsed since then, I have been able to overcome much of this fear, as I have immersed myself more deeply in prayer and reflection on my covenant relationship with God, and in God with those whom I love. I have also experienced a new relationship with my mother since her death, and in a very deep way know that she is living in the closer presence of God.

One of my greatest joys and supports in approaching old age in the Spirit is my life in our community, with brothers of such different ages, and with friends who are closely bound to us here. There are some Christians who either by choice or by circumstances limit their friends to persons of their own age. To live or be in close touch with persons of all ages is a very blessed gift. We who are older have much both to give and to receive in such relationships.

For the older Christian prayer has a special quality, but has also its own difficulties. The older Christian who is seeking to live in the gladness of each day, and who has been faithful in a life of individual prayer, will in all probability be using a rather simple form of affective prayer and will also be able in some degree to transform loneliness into a real aloneness with God. For the older Christian, however, whether as a lay person, a member of a monastic community, or as a priest, there may very likely also be periods of great loneliness and of darkness in prayer, with little or no sense of the presence of God. Such Christians during their more active lives may have found insufficient opportunity for prayer, and so looked forward to a time in their lives when they could devote more time to it. Now they have this time, but feel that their prayer is so feeble, empty, or distracted.

I believe that one explanation to this phenomenon is the fact that their work of ministry or service was a real incentive to their prayer, and that their life of prayer was fed and stimulated by this more active life. Now they have more time for prayer, but less incentive, and often they believe that they no longer are praying at all. If only they will persevere, they will be rewarded by a simpler kind of prayer, simple and affective. For the older Christian living alone, there can be found many opportunities for such prayer, both adoration and intercession. The following quotation from our *Rule of Life* ought to be of real help: "We are to look up to Jesus in the glory of the Father. Although we do not see Him with the outward eye, let us remember that he sees us, and rest in the security of His love. Let us wait till he comes. The vision will surely come. If we persevere in looking to Jesus, he will not fail to give us all we need."

In order to be truly growing old in the Spirit, not just aging, the Christian must accept the limitations which come in the process of becoming physically less active and mentally less alert. She or he will need with the help of others to discern what to hold on to, and what to let go; and then to act in a spirit of real detachment. All of us are familiar with the unhappiness and tension which arise when an older member of a family or community refuses to do so.

To approach old age in the Spirit is, then, to live as totally as possible in the present, seeking to find, to contribute to, to respond to the gladness of each day, and in so doing to thank God for all that he has done for us in the past, and also to look forward without fear to the time of our death. It will not always be easy for us to do so—there will be fear and depression and self-pity to overcome. We can do so, as we respond each day to God's call to follow him in the way of love, a love which he is purifying and deepening—a love which still responds in the circumstances of our daily lives to the call of our Risen Lord to feed his sheep and tend his lambs, and to allow others to feed and tend us in those ways we need. The goal of every Christian is to be transformed into the likeness of Christ, who in the words of St. John of the Cross, "when the evening of our lives comes will judge us by love." If we are faithful to the life of the Spirit, then in the life beyond the grave we, who have spent our lives both in striving and in pressing on to the goal of the prize of Christ Jesus and also in resting in the security of his love, will no longer have to strive because we will have completely found him and be found by him. And so in those magnificent words of St. Augustine,

88

"We shall rest and we shall see, we shall see and we shall love,
we shall love and we shall praise forever and ever, Amen."

Paul Wessinger, SSJE

Cowley Publications is a work of the Society of St. John the
Evangelist, a religious community for men in the Episcopal
Church. The books we publish are a significant part of our ministry, together with the work of preaching, hospitality, and
spiritual direction. Our aim is to provide books that will enrich
their readers' religious experience as well as challenge it with
fresh approaches to religious concerns.